Collecting My Thoughts

by

William G. Carr

Secretary, Educational Policies Commission, 1936-52
Executive Secretary, National Education Association,

1952-67

A Diamond Jubilee Publication of the
Phi Delta Kappa Educational Foundation

Cover design by Victoria Voelker

©1980 William G. Carr
Library of Congress Catalogue Card Number 80-82881
ISBN 0-87367-424-3
Printed in the United States of America

Publication of this monograph has been financed in part through a generous contribution from Miss Bessie Gabbard, a member of the Ohio State University Chapter of Phi Delta Kappa and a member of the Board of Governors of the Phi Delta Kappa Educational Foundation.

Table of Contents

Preface

The essays William Carr has brought together in these pages embody considerably more than a few pleasant and provocative thoughts. What we have in this compact collection is a sampling of the qualities of mind and spirit that have made his contributions to education so distinctive and so influential.

To appreciate more fully the role he has played, we should remember that Dr. Carr's active service with the National Education Association extended from 1929, when he joined its newly formed Research Division, until 1967, when he retired as executive secretary of what had become the country's largest professional organization. The 38 intervening years encompassed the most momentous and critical sequence of events this nation has known in its entire history. The Depression, World War II, the post-war inflation, the Cold War, the Korean action, Sputnik and its aftermath, the population explosion, the *Brown* decision and the civil rights movement, collective bargaining by teachers and the first school strikes, Viet Nam and the student demonstrations of the 1960s. Every one of these events and many others impinged in some way upon American schools. The resulting pressures and tensions required rapid adjustments in curricula, legislation, finance, and management. The seriousness of the problems was widely recognized but few understood them well enough to define them adequately, and fewer still were prepared to offer workable proposals for dealing with them.

To call public attention to the need for educational policy that would respond to the new issues facing the nation and maintain the fundamental principles of American education, the National Education Association and the American Association of School Administrators established in 1937 the Educational Policies Commission. As secretary of the commission from its inception until 1952, Dr. Carr served as its counselor, catalyst, and principal author and was

ix

responsible in large measure for the perceptiveness of its analyses and the sound, far-sighted character of its policy statements. One example among many of the enduring excellence of the commission's work—and his—may be seen in the 1938 report *The Purposes of Education in American Democracy*. Its assessment of the problems and potentiality of American education is as pertinent today as it was when it appeared 42 years ago. In his next post as executive secretary of the National Education Association during the years of its most vigorous growth in membership, professional strength, and public influence, the same qualities of wisdom and sensitivity, combined with impressive administrative skill, gained Dr. Carr national recognition as spokesman for the teaching profession.

Throughout these essays one is reminded repeatedly how much of his success as a leader is explained by his talent as a teacher. By implying more than he explicitly says, he invites and stimulates our own involvement in the subject. He cites a single provocative example, and we find ourselves recalling half a dozen others among our own experiences. He has a knack for putting a question in such a way that we feel uncomfortable if the response that occurs to us is less than rational and just. We have here, in brief, the handiwork of that rare breed of master teacher who first persuades us that we can do better than we thought we could and then inspires us to try.

Not least among the reasons I admire these essays is the tone in which the ideas are presented. Disagreements are expressed without demeaning those who advocate opposing views; opinions are asserted with appropriate vigor, but the arguments are straightforward and they are invariably delivered with restraint and courtesy. I most particularly enjoyed the respite Dr. Carr's prose affords from the turgid, jargon-filled effusions on education that so regularly afflict our field; the lucid, graceful language of these pieces is refreshment for the soul. The contrast is scarcely surprising, however, for as Oliver Wendell Holmes observed long ago, "The style's the man." Readers who know the author will recognize his shadow on these pages; others will find these essays a pleasant introduction to a gentleman well worth knowing.

All of us who work in American education have long been the beneficiaries of William Carr's exceptional gifts. Now we are further indebted to him for this delightful volume—as we are also to Phi Delta Kappa for its decision to publish it.

John H. Fischer
President Emeritus
Teachers College, Columbia University
New York, New York
August, 1980

A Number of Things

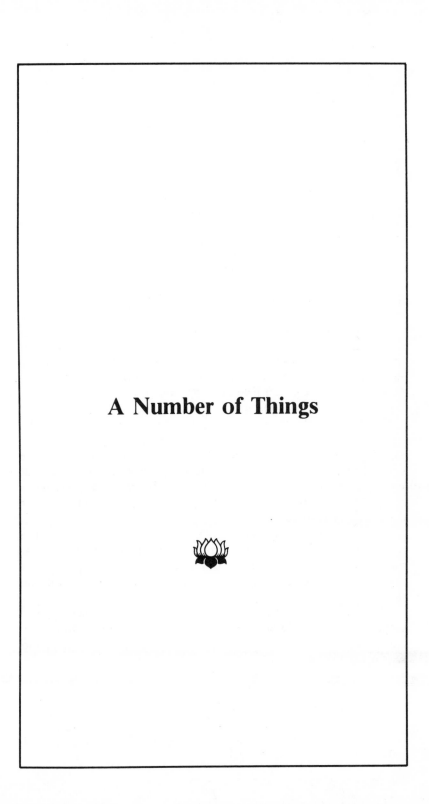

Ceremonies

Rituals and ceremonies serve at least two functions. They simplify life and they enrich it.

Life without ceremony would be vexatious, bewildering, and sluggish. To shake hands with a new acquaintance, to kneel at prayer, to take a posture of respect at a funeral, to salute the passing flag, to rise in the presence of someone highly esteemed—these and a thousand other ceremonial gestures help us to get along with a minimum of friction in a complex, shifting social structure.

When we feel deeply we tend to act uniformly and ceremoniously. Consider commencement exercises. How could these young people casually leave a place that means so much to them? How otherwise could their parents and teachers express what they feel and cannot put into words? Thus the academic procession, the music of *gaudeamus igitur*, the caps and gowns, the reception, the parchments, and the commencement speaker.

What one cannot utter, one may express by a gesture. In spite of its apparent naiveté and starchy formalism, the entire graduation ceremony is really a carefully-staged drama for uniting many people in a common act. Thus emotions are made manageable by generalizing them.

The event also enriches experience. Ceremony lends solemnity and emphasis. It expands horizons, inviting all to examine the shared experience. Thus "standing on ceremony" often elevates us enough to see farther than usual.

Childhood

We like to view childhood as charming, amusing, and amazing—a brief episode of life free of care and subject to delightful adult recollections. Yet when adults gather to consider this most engaging of topics, caution and tension characterize the meeting. Brows furrow in profound cogitation. Our collective adult opinions turn to secret, sad, and guilty forebodings. Talk becomes convoluted and polysyllabic. We make childhood a problem to be solved rather than an experience to be treasured.

Each successive White House Conference on Children, which, by long tradition, is held in Washington every tenth year (I have myself actively participated in five of these decennial spectaculators), sets new records for the profundity of principles uttered, the eloquence of the sentiments expressed, the number of pages of documentation issued, the solemnity of the vows taken, the scope of the resolutions adopted, and the paucity of the concrete results achieved.

In these gatherings a simple and candid statement about our concern for children is a rarity. When such a statement is uttered it clings tightly to the memory. For example, launching the 1930 conference, Herbert Hoover said of children, "We put them to bed with a lingering of devotion and a sense of relief."

But such honest expressions of human interest are rare. Most of what the delegates hear is forgotten before they reach home. The efforts of several thousand people, their abounding enthusiasm, their cultivated skills, and industrious goodwill have produced extremely limited results.

One basic reason for the disparity between effort and achievement is the reticence of most delegates to speak out on controversial issues, *especially where action is necessary.* The penalty for this preference for talking over doing has been the increasing dilution of the effectiveness of White House Conferences on Children. It is likely that 1979, which the United Nations designated "The Year of the Child," has suffered the same verbal drowning.

Clarity

We hold these truths to be self-evident: that all men are created equal, that they are endowed by their Creator with certain unalienable Rights . . . ." How clear and stately are these historic words! Imagine how a draft by a committee of the Society for the Objective Study of Organizations (SO-SO) might read:

"We postulate the following hypotheses as a basis for further objective research, with appropriate controls for the dependent and independent variables, that all observed exemplifications within the parameters of the species *homo sapiens*, when examined under proper experimental conditions, appear to possess identical (or substantially identical) attributes; that an external supermundane Force of omnipotent scope has provided each such specimen with a coalescence of psychologically inseparable prerogatives. . . ." And so on.

Consider another example: Article 2 of the Universal Declaration of Human Rights contains 82 words of which exactly half are polysyllabic. The teachers of the Philippines, being called upon to teach the Universal Declaration to their pupils, neatly paraphrased the Declaration. They rewrote Article 2 in 16 words, a reduction of 80% from the original text and at least 100% more comprehensible.

Few, if any, Thomas Jeffersons are available to serve us today, but there are lots of teachers, in the Philippines and elsewhere, who can (if permitted) help us to express and understand great ideals with clarity.

Duty

Father James Walsh of Georgetown University once published a thorough study of the formal education of the Founding Fathers of the Republic. The men who announced and achieved the independence of the United States and who wrote our Constitution were the product of an education that was centered on ethics, on a moral philosophy for the guidance of life.

Their education stressed duties, not only in their personal lives but also in their conduct as political leaders. In contrast to the schools of today, which teach much about rights and little about responsibilities, much about activism and less about solicitude for the welfare of others, the schools and colleges attended by the Founding Fathers were concerned about the duties of an educated person. They believed, as Tennyson said of the Duke of Wellington, that "the path of duty was the way to glory," and history has shown that their belief was correct.

4

Efficiency

For an individual, a machine, or an organization, efficiency is the ratio of results attained to efforts exerted.

For organizations, at least five factors help to determine their efficiency:

First, the clarity and precision of their stated goals.

Second, periodic measurement of progress toward those goals.

Third, the extent to which the individual members, *as well as the elected leaders and/or employees*, participate in the work to be done. This criterion is far more important than the sheer number of dues-paying members. It accounts for the surprising effectiveness of some small organizations in controlling other organizations that are numerically much larger.

Fourth, flexibility; that is, the capacity to turn quickly to the exploitation of issues when new needs and opportunities arise.

Fifth, and most important, the power to establish priorities among the hundreds of things that are needed or desired (or thought to be so).

Concentration of effort, time, attention, and resources is crucial to efficient management.

Followership

Leaders happen only when people follow. A would-be leader may be absolutely correct in defining the problem and its solution. But there is no leader until others are associated with the proposed program of action.

Successful leadership involves skills, intelligence, knowledge, experience, understanding of human nature—in short, wisdom. But all these admirable qualities are unavailing unless the leader decides and acts. If he will not stand for what he believes, someone else must step forward, shoulder the burden, accept the risk, and *lead*.

In the American setting, followers should be recruited by reason rather than by force or deceit. The informed, competent, enthusiastic follower is, in essence, the ultimate source of leadership.

Leaders are supposed to look forward, but they must also glance backward from time to time to make sure others are behind them. The wisest person who makes the most far-sighted decision remains a prophet and is not a leader until there are followers.

The first person to reach the meeting place is not a leader, no matter how many people enter afterwards. The leader is not created by priority, by good intentions, or by an honorary title. The first person on the scene is the leader only if others came because he did, if they remain because he stands fast.

Foreboding

The tendency to emulate Cassandra prognosticating woe and to predict the decline and fall of mankind is a recurrent epidemic. Examples are almost endless. In 1857 the Ohio State Department of Education made the gloomy forecast:

> None can doubt that feebleness of body is more general than it was . . . Deterioriation has progressed so as to alarm every thoughtful mind. The children of this country are becoming every year less healthful and good-looking. . . . Poor health is so very common among grown people, especially women. Physicians fear ere long there will be no more healthy women in the country.

Such lugubrious forecasts are usually accompanied by an appeal to return to the "good old days." Some 50 years ago Professor William Lyons Phelps wrote in despair: "Family discipline is weak; the child rules the house; the family obeys his caprices."

The undisciplined children, described by Professor Phelps as ruling and ruining the home, now possess grown children of their own. They mourn because, they say, their grandchildren lack that wholesome discipline which, they wrongly believe, ennobled and enriched their own childhood.

Crying "Wolf!" is still a favorite occupation. It is, however, worth remembering that in the fable the wolf really did come at last, and the flock and the shepherd were destroyed together.

Indoctrination

In prosperity and depression, in war and peace, the word "indoctrination" can, when uttered, produce a vigorous debate in any educational assembly. Such discussions, if they reach any conclusion at all, are apt to conclude with a tidy formula: "The public schools should teach how to think, not what to think."

This conclusion has an apparent sweet reasonableness, but it will not work in practice. For one thing, it assumes that "how to think" can be taught and learned without regard to the content of the thinking. Any subject of thought, any compilation of evidence about ideas, are sure to reflect the interests, values, and opinions of teachers and textbook writers who select and present that information.

Should the schools have an explicit policy to study controversial issues? Should they teach the basic objectives of American society and government? Should they offer a choice from a broad range of answers to controversial issues? These three questions suggest three different kinds of indoctrination: indoctrination for procedure, for social objectives, and for social programs. Which of these three, if any, is an appropriate form of indoctrination for the schools?

No simple formula can resolve these solid problems once and forever.

Inertia

Motivation powerful enough to bring about real change must be both resourceful and persistent. The natural enemies of a new idea are varied, ubiquitous, and lethal. I have myself experienced and counted at least 10 formulas to murder a new proposal. Here they are:

1. Let's not be stampeded into hasty decisions.
2. This proposal has not been discussed by all those concerned.
3. This is a halfway measure, leaving the root of the problem unchanged.
4. This revolutionary scheme is fraught with unpredictable consequences.
5. Let's give present policies a chance to work. Why dig up the carrots every day to see whether they are growing?
6. Let's refer the question to a committee or a task force.
7. This proposal would establish a bad precedent if applied elsewhere.
8. This is the thin edge of an entering wedge or the first step on a slippery slope.
9. A splendid suggestion! But the time is not right.
10. No quorum is present.

Entangled in the meshes of the above web, only a very good idea, applied to a really desperate situation, has a chance of survival. Otherwise inertia will make sure that the thought is not father of the deed.

Inflation

Politicians solemnly assure us that inflation is very bad. Most of us already know that but we applaud the speeches anyway. If we listen carefully we are likely to hear some remarkable information about the inflationary impact of certain expenditures.

For example, federal funds to improve schools are especially inflationary. But state and local spending to improve schools are commendable and will not produce inflation.

The cost of operating a car is rising 15% a year, but transportation is a necessity, isn't it?

Large-scale national expenditures to explore space, to develop new weapons, or to increase the size of the defense establishment are not inflationary because they are already in The Budget. But the cost of preparing young people to live in the Space Age is highly inflationary because it is not in The Budget.

So, if the purchasing power of your life insurance or your pension is cut in half by inflation, you can blame all your consequent misfortunes on the importunate demands of the power-hungry teachers' lobby!

Have you heard about the thief who broke into a car at the shopping center? He stole fifty dollars' worth of groceries—took them right out of the glove compartment. That's what comes of reckless spending for schools.

Insularity

When high school graduates move into the wider community, their interest in civic affairs often deteriorates. Why do the bright ideals of youth fade into common day?

Many schools are like islands, set apart from the mainland by a moat of tradition. A drawbridge, lowered twice a day, permits the students to reach their island in the morning and to return home at night.

Why do the youth go to the island? To learn how to live on the mainland. To this end, well-illustrated books about the mainland are provided on the island.

To promote maximum learning, the island must be a controlled environment. There is little justification for a school that is just as bad as the community that surrounds it. However, if control of the island's environment completely insulates school from community, the control defeats its own purpose.

In the late afternoon the janitors take charge of the island. By evening the drawbridge is up and silent darkness is relieved only by the sweeping of the janitor and the flashlight of the watchman. The island is lifeless most of Saturday and Sunday. The drawbridge collects cobwebs all summer and during other long holidays.

One evening a year the island's lights burn late. This event is called graduation. After that the islanders depart, never to set foot on the island again. Such, only slightly caricatured, is the insularity of many American schools.

After the graduates leave the island for the last time, they are bombarded by problems of life on the mainland. Sometimes, struggling with these new preoccupations, one of the graduates may mutter, "On the island I read something about that problem in a book."

8

Leadership

The real test of leadership happens only in an emergency, only where a difficult choice is to be made. Several courses of action will be open and each will have its devoted advocates. No controversy, no decision; no decision, no leadership. Even if the leader chooses a compromise or proposes a plebiscite, the fiercest partisans will be unsatisfied. Leadership is a hazardous occupation; taking chances is its business.

When no great issues divide public opinion, when the calm course of events is unruffled by the gales of controversy, there is no place of consequence for leadership. Only when violence tugs at the leash of reason, when minds are shaken by doubts and darkened by despair can great leadership flourish. When people stand perplexed at a parting of the ways, when many good reasons can be given for taking this road or that, the true leader is one who steps forward and chooses a way to go.

Leadership *in education* is a specialized instance of these general rules. The slowly accumulated gains of civilization are perpetually and precariously balanced on the knife-edge that separates one generation from another. A single badly-taught generation could and would squander the cultural savings of a 1000 years of social evolution. Against ignorance, apathy, and malice, the remorseless enemies of all beautiful and holy things, education wages a continuous and, at best, a doubtful battle.

The qualities of leadership for that battle are the courage to choose, the wisdom to choose rightly, and the patient persuasion to enlist followers. Under such leadership the profession of education continues the struggle, not with the thought that it will be won in this generation or the next or the next, but with the assurance that to give battle to such enemies is, in itself, a notable victory and that the zest of the conflict is its own priceless reward.

Maturity

In 1963 John Gardner wrote a very good book titled *Self-Renewal*. It's message is, in essence, a method of maturing without the disadvantages of old age.

As with individuals, so also with institutions. If they survive they become acquisitive. Institutions acquire furniture, inventories, national offices, regional offices, personnel policies, handbooks, guidelines, by-laws, long-term commitments, status, and reputations. Their acquisitions weigh them down like leaden shoes. Responsibility to the valued heritage of the past creates caution. People who travel light are more venturesome; they have less to risk and less to lose. Most of us are owned by our possessions.

Thus, institutions grow chiefly by addition—another staff member, another conference, another committee, another newsletter. To grow by accretion is much easier than to grow by self-renewal.

Everyone wishes to be thought young; no one wishes to be called immature. Maturity made frontier towns safer, more healthful, more pleasant. It also made them harder to change.

Any person who has shared in building a new institution recalls with nostalgia the early days of impossible ambitions, of happy confusion, and of soaring morale. But few of us with such memories are really prepared to return to the primitive level of the past recalled with fond inaccuracy.

Morale

M orale is a state of mind marked by courage and confidence. It is not to be confused with a slack assurance that success will come without effort or pain, nor with a sudden surge of adrenalin-spiked energy.

As discipline is the basic psychology of the drill-master, so morale is the basis of successful leadership.

The sources of morale are not fully understood, but it seems clear that morale is evoked by the respect of others and by self-respect. It is the voluntary acceptance of mutually agreed on standards of conduct.

Morale thrives on useful employment. Enforced idleness is its worst enemy. Well-founded trust in leaders and colleagues maintains morale. Better, as far as morale is concerned, to suffer an occasional disappointment than to endure the misery of continued suspicion.

Reasonably good health is necessary for good morale. Poor diet, infection, or extreme fatigue, if unrelieved, usually destroy morale. Yet, under stress and strong motivation, sick and weary people sometimes respond surprisingly well.

Honest presentation of adverse factors builds morale. Winston Churchill, in the darkest days of World War II, offered the British people nothing, he said, but "blood, toil, tears, and sweat" and their morale soared.

Optimism

Norman Thomas, venerated leader of the U.S. Socialist Party, spent most of his life in vigorous denunciation of the policies of the United States, foreign and domestic. Yet he found time and inclination to interrupt the flood of his censure with an eloquent article on what was right about his country. In the midst of a life-long crusade for radical change, he paused long enough to record those things he admired.

Such a pause refreshes. It is an especially wholesome prescription for the teaching profession which, more than most occupations, is loudly, restlessly, and severely self-critical. Racked by an insatiable discontent, educators normally describe their calling as one forever on the brink of dreadful catastrophe. Only some swift and epochal reform, they believe, can avert disaster. The idea that teachers as a group are tradition-bound and self-laudatory is about as far from truth as fancy can stray. If you doubt this, listen in the back row at at any teacher's meeting.

In our eternal struggle to remake the present and avert the threat of the future, we would do well to take time occasionally to emulate Norman Thomas, count our blessings, gloat over past achievements, and proclaim the virtues of the pleasant present.

Personnel

Just imagine a situation in which the superintendent tried to do personally all the work involved in running a school system. Such behavior would be correctly regarded as demented. At the minimum, a corps of teachers and, in most school systems, principals, supervisors, research workers, attendance officers, business managers, and other specialists are required.

All these assistants make the superintendent's task manageable. They also entail a series of difficult personnel problems. Human relations are complicated, calling for patience, tact, generosity, courage, firmness, honesty, and whatever other virtues are at hand.

The material assets of a school can be treated arbitrarily and roughly. A chair will serve almost as well in one place as in another. If broken, it can be replaced. The human assets of a school are, however, diverse and perishable. A is angered by P's promotion to the principalship. T does well as a teacher in Grade III and barely gets by in Grade VIII. Dilatory D comes late to work while eager E wants to leave early to take an extension course. R feels that retirement at age 65 deprives the schools of his services just as they are reaching their maturity—and besides, he needs the income and the satisfactions of active work. The entire staff demands an upward revision of the salary schedule while a new school board member insists that salaries should be related to the quality of teaching.

To manage even a few such conflicts is a source of great professional satisfaction. Good teachers do not come to a school system by accident nor do they remain by inertia. All the other machinery of the school system falters without a devoted and capable staff. That is why personnel policy is the top priority of successful administration.

Perspective

Some aircraft lately have been equipped with a useless and costly device that enables passengers to view on a screen the runway speeding below them as their plane rises into flight. I find the view from the cabin window far more instructive.

When a plane takes off, there comes a moment of uncertainty whether it is still earthbound or newly airborne. At this moment, just as the wheels leave the surface, the passenger sees the land fall away beneath him and he begins to gain a new perspective on objects previously seen only at ground level.

On the ground, the jumble of streets seemed to be merely an annoying source of delay and a meaningless confusion of movement, noise, and directions. From the air the masses of buildings and the flow of traffic come into relationship. The shape of the city emerges. The main avenues display their purposeful pattern. Large edifices stand out clearly—they could not be seen at ground level because smaller buildings blocked the view. As one rises higher, the city within its environs emerges—perhaps a harbor, the course of a river, or a crinkly expanse of white-edged sea. One literally sees "how the land lies."

Such an experience, applied to the examination of any other phenomenon, enables us to "rise above" the daily confusion of detail to see, as we put it, "the larger picture." The bird's eye view in all matters helps us to see how things really are in perspective.

Practice

The United Nations and such specialized agencies as Unesco are tools. When people ask if the UN is working, I am tempted to ask them in reply whether a spade works. A spade works only when someone digs with it.

Suppose a friend approaches me, hands me a violin and says, "It's time to relax. Please play a tune on this violin."

I would have to say, "A good idea, but I never learned to play a violin; it looks rather complicated."

My friend might persist, saying, "See what a splendid violin I offer you. The best violin makers in San Francisco worked on it for months, using the finest wood, glue, and other materials."

I would have to respond, "Sorry; it makes no difference how good the instrument is. Since I have not learned how to use it, I can produce nothing but discordant noise."

But if my friend had approached, instead of me, a Fritz Kreisler and offered him a five-dollar fiddle picked up at the corner pawnshop, Kreisler could make sweet music to charm your heart out. True, he could make even better music with a better instrument—and we should get him the best we can—but the crucial fact is that *he knows how; he has learned.*

One great task of education is to teach youth how to use the instruments of international relations which we have built as best we could. Unless children acquire the tools of learning and practice persistently, nothing else they learn is likely to be of lasting value.

Pressures

Alexis de Tocqueville, early in the last century, devoted a chapter of his *Democracy in America* to explaining our "civil societies," as he called them. The variety, power, and prestige of such societies continue to grow. If we like their aims they are "voluntary public service organizations"; if we don't like them they are "pressure groups."

By whatever name, these groups promote their objectives in more powerful ways than by merely participating in the election of school board members and legislators. The American Legion, the Urban League, the Better Business Bureau, the American Federation of Labor, the Daughters of the American Revolution, and countless others press their respective and often incompatible views on the schools. They organize contests, drives, collections, exhibits, sit-ins, walk-outs, special days, special weeks, and anniversaries that run all year. They form caucuses and mount confrontations. They demand that the schools give more attention to (for instance) first aid, little league baseball, mental hygiene, speech correction, Spanish in the primary grades, international understanding, world history, Black history, American history, local history, sex-role stereotypes, the Arabs and the Israelis, Christopher Columbus and/or Leif Ericson, nutrition, care of the teeth, free enterprise, labor relations, cancer prevention, atomic energy, dental hygiene, the use of firearms, the Constitution, evils of tobacco, temperance, kindness to animals, Esperanto, use of the typewriter, legible penmanship, digital computers, moral values, fire prevention, physical fitness, thrift, religious liberty, law observance, consumerism, narcotics, mathematics, dramatics, physics, ceramics, phonics, politics, and safe bicycling.

Each group wants to avoid overloading the curriculum. All any of them ask is that non-essentials be dropped in order to get their material in. Most of them do not ask for a special course—they just want their ideas to permeate the daily program for 12 years.

It is the uncontested privilege of American citizens to fashion their schools to meet their needs. Some of our most widely accepted educational services entered the schools by this route. Nevertheless, the pressure system grows less manageable daily. How school administrators deal with such public pressures in some kind of orderly fashion remains a nearly insoluble problem.

Professions

Many attempts have been made to differentiate between the professions and the other vocations. Many of these attempts, I fear, have been unproductive and misleading.

I conclude that a profession is an occupation in which the service rendered is regarded, *by the worker*, more highly than the personal pecuniary rewards it brings. It is not some characteristic of the occupation itself that makes it professional; it is the attitude of the worker to the work.

A carpenter more interested in doing excellent carpentry than in making more money is a professional carpenter.

A physician more interested in becoming rich than in healing is a non-professional laborer.

Other criteria have been proposed but they all collapse in application. It is said, for example, that a profession requires long preparation. Is a teacher who has graduated from a one-year normal school less professional than one with a Ph.D. degree? The question cannot even be argued intelligently until we observe what motivates each of them.

It has been said that a profession involves the use of mental processes rather than manual dexterity. By this criterion a train dispatcher is a professional and an ophthalmic surgeon is not.

Thus the basic element in a profession, competence being assumed in all cases, is a strong sense of public responsibility.

Recess

In 1885 the National Education Association held its annual meeting in Saratoga, New York. Influenced perhaps by the health spa at which they met, the delegates gave attention to a number of factors related to pupils' health.

The NEA Standing Committee on Hygiene considered the school recess as a health measure. A sampling of professional opinion showed that a slight majority favored a no-recess policy. One speaker pointed to the dangers of exposure to cold, the waste of time in passing in and out of the building, and the perils of mud in the school yard. Others rejoined that the air in classrooms becomes poisonous and recess provides needed fresh air.

The recess opponents said that their policy would enable children and teachers to go home earlier. The children could then play at home under parental supervision. Another opponent of recess estimated that in ordinary recess one-eighth of the children exercised vigorously while the rest inhaled the dust created by the active ones.

One contributor to the debate said that recess for 100 teen-age boys would surely be marked by personal injuries and the learning of profanity. The St. Louis school superintendent, however, said he would rather trust 500 boys together than two or three, and that the best playground supervision was provided by the pupils themselves.

The discussion continued with vigor for some time. To end it, the president of NEA declared that decisions about recess would depend on local conditions—a "cop-out" that is used in educational debates even today.

Retirement

Every year, almost every business, corporation, school system, college, or government agency loses some of its most experienced personnel through involuntary retirement.

Farewell dinners are organized. There are repeated rounds of applause and prolonged speeches of appreciation. Lumps rise in certain throats and some eyes moisten while junior staff members silently estimate the opportunities for advancement that the impending departures may create.

Since past and continuing inflation renders the pensions and savings of many retired persons insufficient to maintain their previous living standards, many of them seek and accept other work. This post-retirement employment is usually of less social value than the work they did before the flip of a calendar page cast them out. The economic waste, overall, is substantial; the human waste is appalling.

Those who want to quit work at 65 should be permitted (and sometimes encouraged) to do so. Uniform compulsory retirement at a stated age does avoid numerous administrative difficulties. But at what cost! Why should society reject services that experienced workers are eager and competent to provide? The ancient astrologers called 3 and 9 magic numbers, but who can establish a talismanic value for 65 or 70?

Salutes

In the midst of World War II, the U.S. Supreme Court made one of its sudden reversals of opinion. In 1940 the Court had upheld the exclusion from schools of pupils who refused to comply with flag salute regulations. In 1943 the Court took the opposite opinion. In both cases there were dissenting minority opinions.

"Free public education," the Court declared in the 1943 ruling, "if faithful to the ideal of secular instruction or political neutrality, will not be partisan or enemy of any class, creed, party, or faction. . . . Compulsory unification of opinion achieves only the unanimity of the graveyard."

Fundamental human rights, the Court concluded, are not subject to ratification or denial, even by plebiscite.

The Court refused to assume that patriotism could not flourish without a compulsory routine. It is an unflattering estimate of the appeal of our free institutions to suppose that love of this country cannot be evoked by patriotic ceremonies that are voluntary and spontaneous.

That is still the law today and it still makes sense.

Security

The two basic elements of national security are materiel and manpower. Each element stands at the end of a long chain of contributing factors.

Materiel depends ultimately on resources. Education can neither augment nor diminish the natural raw materials of the United States, but it does contribute significantly to their discovery, conservation, and use. Years of basic and technical education provide metallurgists, soil conservation experts, geologists, foresters, agronomists, and others skilled in the extractive industries.

The road from raw materials to finished products is a long one. From pit to ore-boat to smelter to foundry to forge to factory to machine shop to shipping room requires skilled workers at every stage. Only part of their training is provided by the schools, but systematic schooling can organize the competence in language, number, and human relations from which a developing technology arises.

As for manpower, whether one considers health, vocational effectiveness, or civic loyalty, the role of the school is sometimes central, always important. If basic schooling were to be impaired or interrupted, the adverse results might not be instantly apparent. For a short interval there might be no evident diminution of effectiveness. But soon, as certain and as devastating as an explosion set off by a long fuse, the nation would find itself unable to function.

General Eisenhower said, "To neglect our school system . . . could well be more disastrous to all our freedoms than the most formidable assault on our physical defenses." That is expert testimony on national security.

Sputnik

In October 1957 the Soviet Union launched Sputnik, the first man-made earth satellite. Thus the American public discovered that the Russians were capable of some substantial technical skills.

The first American reaction was hysteria interspersed by panic. After about three months in shock, a period of massive fault-finding ensued. The schools were almost unanimously selected as the chief culprit to be held responsible for the awkward fact that the Soviet Union had a satellite and we had none. The White House, the Congress, the engineering colleges, the scientific community, the Pentagon—all escaped blameless. Many accusing fingers pointed at the schools and few hands were extended to help them.

After the finger-pointers had enjoyed about six months of happy scapegoating, the United States launched its Explorer, a satellite that went up and stayed up. We discovered that Explorer had been planned and built in a hurry primarily by people who had graduated from American public high schools. Then these same people put up a satellite that not only beeped but wished the world a Merry Christmas. Soon we had more artificial moons than the Russians. But Admiral Hyman Rickover, Professor Arthur Bestor, and the Luce publications refused to be comforted. Our satellites were too small and they didn't have a dog in them and it was all the fault of the schools.

Twelve years after Sputnik, Americans walked on the moon and returned safely to tell about it.

Did anyone say then that perhaps our schools were not as bad as they had been pictured? Of course not! Don't ask silly questions!

Surprises

A t the outset of World War II, Singapore was regarded as an unconquerable naval base. Yet the Japanese Army drove south through Malaya and took the British fortress with astonishing ease and rapidity.

In his memoirs Churchill recalls that the Japanese were almost at the gates before it was realized that Singapore's cannon could not be used effectively against an invasion from the north. Whoever designed the defenses of Singapore must have "known" that an assault could come only from the sea.

The result of this situation was the loss of the greatest naval base in Asia, the capture of a substantial British Army, the sinking of two of the largest battleships in the fleet, and a serious prolongation of the war in the Pacific. Many similar stories illustrate the drama of the unexpected.

It is a wise person, indeed, who can anticipate the problems that will confront American society 50 years from now. Yet much of our schooling is conducted as though such prediction is possible. Perhaps the greatest blessing education can bestow is the ability to cope with change and thus to deal with the surprises of science and technology.

It is proper that education deal with current issues. It is even better that education develop principles that can be applied to whatever surprises lurk in the shrouded future.

Time

Most people give close attention in labor negotiations to comparisons about the time we spend at work. We gravely discuss annual leave, sick leave, hours of employment. We would be wise to spend at least as much energy thinking about the rest of our time—our time of rest.

None of us will ever have any more time than we have right now. We each have all the time there is. No one can steal your time. Your time is your time; no one can even borrow your time without your consent and active assistance. This is one valuable commodity delivered fresh to each of us every morning with perfect equality.

Time is supplied to all at an unvarying and uniform rate. We cannot spend it in advance. The next minute, the next hour, the next year is as fully at your disposal as though you had never wasted a single moment of your life.

Most of us spend at work, or in closely related activity, about 45 hours a week. We sleep, on average, about 55 hours a week. Total for work and sleep 100 hours. Aha! Seven times 24 equals 168 hours. The difference is 68 hours, a time considerably greater than either work or sleep. What we do with those 68 hours determines largely the kind of person we become. Few of us can account for those 68 hours. Perhaps it is just as well; if we could account for them, the results would probably be very depressing.

Time is our primary resource. We should try to conserve it for it is irreplaceable.

Victory

There is not a fiercer Hell than failure in a great project," wrote Keats in his preface to *Endymion*. But there *is* a more cruel fate than Keats acknowledged. It is to achieve victory and see its fruits wasted.

Defeat is indeed a searching test of character, but victory makes even sterner demands. The most demanding test, for an individual or an institution, is not recovery from defeat but the constructive exploitation of success. The responsible use of the fruits of victory is usually more difficult than victory itself.

All activity, individual or corporate, is directed toward a purpose. That is why, as soon as a goal is achieved, a new or extended goal must be quickly fashioned to fill the gap created by victory. This may be one reason why wars won on the battlefield seem too often to be lost at the peace table.

When, after exhausting effort, after the prolonged painful adaptations of tactics to resources, victory at last is grasped, the supreme test then faces the victor. After the excitement of the conflict is stilled, after the cheers of the victory celebration have subsided, a new kind of strength is required. All the traits that led to victory in the first place—clarity of purpose, intelligent compromise, unwavering determination—all are still needed in the post-victory period. Magnanimity is needed so that defeated opponents may be induced to help in the tasks ahead.

Fortunate are they who, in the midst of all-out conflict, find some corner of the mind to plan the uses of the success they seek.

Wastebaskets

The cost of equipment for advanced study and research has become staggering. Universities no longer operate merely with a judicious selection of books and journals. The sciences, on the whole, make the most extravagant demands for equipment and supplies. The equipment for medical schools is also very expensive.

There are some consolations. The theoretical mathematicians, the literary critics, and the philosophers may be made quite happy with a supply of writing paper, pencils, and wastebaskets. Indeed, some of them seem to feel no need for the wastebasket.

The computer is an expensive item of educational equipment that is useful in many disciplines. It is essentially a means of storing and supplying new arrangements of data. Inevitably and unfortunately, the capacity of the computer to arrange and present data outruns by far the ability of human beings to use the added information. Like the ever-running salt-mill in Grimm's fairy tale, the computer insists on delivering multitudinous seas of data—more than we want, more than we need, more than we can use.

The wastebasket not used by the philosophy department should, I suggest, be turned over to the computer people. The prudent use of the wastebasket is the key to a happy symbiosis between academic humanity and the electronic computer.

A Few Good People

Ada Ashley

Not much is known about Mrs. Ada Ashley who, during World War II, taught in a rural school near Lebanon, Missouri. She served on no important national committees, wrote no widely-used textbook, made no outstanding contributions to pedagogical theory. We do not know what academic degrees she held, if any.

One thing we do know: Mrs. Ahsley, according to the Associated Press, trudged by night along the by-roads of her school district until she had visited every home in it. Her mission: to collect money for the Red Cross. Her journey: roughly 100 miles, all on foot. Her collections: 25 dollars, mostly in small change.

Nothing spectacular, nothing very risky. Good for one line in an AP dispatch on a slow day. One more example of the everlasting importance of the individual citizen. It was the Mrs. Ashleys of America who won the war. They will continue to smash ignorance, indifference, and inertia in whatever form they appear. There are millions of Mrs. Ashleys and none of them will receive a medal, or be asked to sit on the platform, or be awarded degrees *honoris causa* from learned institutions.

Someone was needed to collect money for the Red Cross. Mrs. Ashley didn't say "Why me?" or "I don't drive," or "I'm busy." She just went out and did her duty. If she knew about the AP story, she was probably astounded that anyone thought her effort worth recording. But it was.

James B. Conant

As a chemist, he assumed heavy public responsibility for the production of synthetic rubber when our supply of natural rubber was cut off by the Japanese occupation of Southeast Asia.

As a scientist, he performed important secret work in the Manhattan Project for the atomic weapon that brought about the Japanese surrender.

As a diplomat, he represented his country in the most difficult years of postwar Germany.

As the president of Harvard University, 1933-53, he bore an immense administrative and intellectual responsibility for the nation's oldest and most distinguished institution of higher learning.

Other men, laden with such multiplied duties, have ignored the problems of elementary and secondary education. Dr. Conant, however, devoted long, steadfast, and profound attention to the public schools. Because he chose to do so, the schools are much better—and would be better still if some of his modestly proposed advice had been more often heeded.

His dogged support of the principle of equal opportunity in education was the keystone of his faith in education as indispensable to American democracy. No American since Thomas Jefferson has perceived this relationship more clearly or expressed it more vigorously, consistently, and persuasively to the American people.

James W. Crabtree

In 1917 James William Crabtree was elected executive secretary of the National Education Association. His first decision was to move the small office from his home in Peru, Nebraska, to Washington, D.C.

He could then count on about 10,000 dues-paying members. When he retired two decades later, the membership had risen to 200,000. During those years the NEA *Journal* was inaugurated, a Research Division was created, moribund committees were revitalized, and the participation of the members in the work of the Association was greatly increased. All these things were done so unobtrusively that those who now use NEA services assume that they have existed automatically since the beginning of time.

The NEA had no permanent headquarters in Washington. Everyone wistfully deplored that fact. But Crabtree decided to secure the necessary capital by promoting life membership. His most sophisticated colleagues regarded the proposal as a mirage, but he trusted the teachers to respond to strong leadership. In 1932 the NEA dedicated a new seven-story office building to the service of the teaching profession. Mr. Crabtree happily survived to witness the ceremonial burning of the mortgage in 1935.

He was a quiet man, painfully modest, a man who believed from the experience of his own youth that education could lift us all out of ignorance and poverty. He always worked with his office door open and, more important, with his mind and heart open. Millions of teachers and children, although they never saw his face or heard his name, enjoyed better schools and better lives because James Crabtree trusted the American dream.

Ellwood P. Cubberley

For almost a half-century up to 1933, thousands of students were taught and influenced by Ellwood Patterson Cubberley, dean of the School of Education at Stanford University. Most of those students became influential leaders in American education. What they learned from Dean Cubberley is important to the current status of the public schools.

He taught us first the relation between effective schools and popular government. In his classes on the history of education he showed how democratic ideals and public schools developed together. The public schools, he said, embodied "the distant hopes of statesmen and reformers." The old aristocracy, short-sighted politicians, the ignorant, and the penurious feared that public schools would "educate people out of their proper position." He taught us how these forces were overcome, how the stigma of charity was banished from the schools, how state supervision was established, how the schools were saved from religious sectarianism, and how the public high schools and state universities eventually crowned the system.

Second, he taught us that schools must adapt to new conditions. He taught diligently, although we have not always remembered, that the true purpose of the public school is not to preserve all things unchanged, but rather to anticipate and help to solve individual and social problems.

Third, he showed us that education offers a good career for competent, well-prepared people.

He taught these three lessons to all his students. Indirectly, however, through his students and his writings Dr. Cubberley's quiet voice reached far beyond Room 55, his classroom on the sunny Stanford inner quadrangle. The American people became his audience and their children his clients.

Lyndon B. Johnson

From George Washington onwards, each President of the United States has affirmed that democratic government requires an enlightened citizenry, that national prosperity depends on learning to work productively, and that the general welfare requires citizens who have been taught the moral and spiritual values in which American civilization is rooted.

So they said, and doubtless meant it. President Lyndon Baines Johnson, however, far more than any of the others, translated these concerns into specific legislative proposals. Then he pushed and cajoled Congress to enact them. Once the laws were enacted, he saw to their faithful execution with great vigor.

His administration remains unique in the scope, variety, and long-range importance of legislation on education. The new laws increased educational opportunity for all persons, ranging from the least privileged preschool child in Head Start through the primary and high schools, to youths and adults seeking vocational training, and to graduate students in the professions and the arts. In a period of four years and 10 months he signed 60 new public laws for the improvement of education.

Through all his many years of political service in Washington, he carefully preserved the document which showed that he was a teacher on leave of absence from the public schools of Texas. He would produce and proudly display that document on the least provocation. He left office with the unusual distinction of being an honorary life member of the National Education Association, happy to have been designated as "The Teacher in the White House."

Danny Kaye

To lose one's passport to the land of childhood is one of the penalties for growing up. Few escape the penalty, but Danny Kaye's passport has not been lifted. Like the Pied Piper of Hamelin, his special sorcery reaches the hearts of children everywhere.

The stolid burghers of Hamelin watched dumbfounded as the Pied Piper played and

> All the little boys and girls
> With rosy cheeks and flaxen curls
> And sparkling eyes and teeth like pearls
> Tripping and skipping ran merrily after
> The wonderful music with shouting and laughter.

Both the Pied Piper and Danny Kaye are magicians—but with this difference: the Piper made children disappear whereas Danny Kaye makes us see them more clearly. Not all children have sparkling eyes and skipping feet. Millions of them are in dreadful need, abandoned by their families and by us all, tormented by disease, crippled by illiteracy and hunger.

Under the banner of the United Nations (UNICEF), Danny Kaye has conducted not a new Children's Crusade but a Crusade for Children. He travelled a million miles to bring love and laughter to children. His filmed reports have raised millions of dollars for UNICEF. He writes about it, plugs it on his TV programs, and in 1965 went to Oslo for that shining moment when UNICEF was awarded the Nobel Peace Prize.

He has become a master teacher, using his hands and his heart, his head and his dancing feet, his words and his equally expressive gestures to make us understand that what happens to children affects us all.

Joy E. Morgan

For 34 years Joy Elmer Morgan edited the *Journal* of the National Education Association. Through its pages, his ideas reached more teachers than those of any other educator at any time in U.S. history. His name will always be associated with great enterprises which he promoted in its pages:

American Education Week which since 1921 has brought millions of citizens to visit their schools every year.

The *NEA Handbook* and the *American Citizen's Handbook* were his inventions.

His Horace Mann Centennial (1937) for the first time drew wide public attention to a great American and his advocacy for the public school system.

The Victory Action Program (1942) mobilized the public schools for their war-time efforts.

After the war, the NEA Centennial Program created long-range planning for that event in 1957.

He lifted the quality of educational journalism and made the NEA the world's largest publisher of materials for and about education.

Three qualities made such a career possible: 1) a special ability to give practical effect to an intense idealism; 2) a capacity to focus his energies, almost ferociously, on immediate programs with long-term goals; and 3) an organization to keep moving forward at all times, testing new methods and goals while resisting diversions.

Oh, Joy, the best tribute to your work would be some modern imitators, however feeble.

Johann Heinrich Pestalozzi

Most educators who attain fame do so by writing books rather than by their demonstrated prowess in actual teaching. Pestalozzi (1746-1827) was a towering exception to the rule. He was one of those regrettably rare individuals who could not only write clear and energetic prose about the teaching-learning process but also dedicate his days to the active and successful practice of teaching.

His example, his perceptions about the nature of learning, are as worthy of recognition in today's America as they were two centuries ago when Pestalozzi and his devoted wife, Anna, began in Neuhof to teach the most neglected and deprived children of poor Swiss peasants.

Pestalozzi's solicitude for the underprivileged, his conviction that education is concerned with moral principles as well as with knowledge, his adamant refusal to separate the school from the rest of the child's life, his faith in the possibilities of goodness in human nature—all of these ideas retain a central position in educational debate today.

It is doubtful whether any other foreign educator has exerted on American education today an influence so benign, so profound, and so enduring.

William F. Russell

When we were very young, most of us were taught to say, "Thank you!" Our mothers admonished us:

Be sure to thank Mrs. White for the nice party.
Write a thank-you note to Aunt Mary for your new gloves.
What do you say to Uncle George for the coloring book?

How hard the lesson! How often with averted eyes and reluctant steps did we try to avoid it! Even when we are grown, the well-coached lesson of youth often remains unapplied. Thus, like children still, we postpone the grateful gesture until the more convenient time that never quite arrives.

For once at least, in April 1955, my wife and I broke the habit; we gave quite a large dinner to express our gratitude to Dr. William Fletcher Russell.

First, for his services in civic education. He directed the citizenship program of the Justice Department in World War II. In 1939 he organized the International Congress on Citizenship which steadied the vision and steeled the nerves of the Free World for the ordeal ahead of it.

Second, for his leadership in international education. Although already laden with the highest honors of foreign governments, Dr. Russell accepted the presidency of the struggling new World Organization of the Teaching Profession. The position involved six years of punishing hard work without compensation and with little public recognition. His responsibilities included years of difficult negotiations, always at considerable personal inconvenience and often, for Dr. Russell, in pain and sickness.

Finally, as deputy director of the Foreign Operations Administration for President Eisenhower, Dr. Russell devoted his profound insight and elastic enthusiasm to the end that education might contribute to the progress of the developing nations.

Ole Sand

In 1963 I appointed Ole Sand to direct the new NEA Center for the Study of Instruction. Nothing more important happened during my tenure as NEA Executive Secretary. Ole Sand made a future-oriented policy normal procedure in American education.

In 1973, during a conference in New Orleans, Ole Sand took a short walk. He either stumbled or was pushed so that his head struck the pavement, causing a concussion and coma from which he never emerged.

Three traits won Ole Sand immense respect and affection all his short life.

First, a sense of time. Let me illustrate. When an infant wants something he wants it instantly. A demonstration of outrage usually follows even a slight delay. An adolescent who must wait a few days regards the delay as an agonizing eternity. Maturity consists, in large part, of achieving a sense of time. Such maturity enabled Ole Sand to think comfortably about the schools of the 1980s without the dizzy disorientation produced by the premature arrival of the future.

Second, a capacity for noncombative discourse. In discussions he encountered no opponents, only partners in a common effort to find the best way. To other people, as to himself, he applied the proverb of his Nordic ancestors: "To improve the world, first sweep your doorstep."

Third, a delightful wit. He did not seek the big guffaw. His wit made the listener chuckle for a moment and then think for an hour.

How we all wish he could have stayed with us longer! "In life, as on the stage," wrote Cicero, "it is not necessary that an actor's part shall continue until the conclusion of the drama; it is sufficient in whatever scene he makes his exit—that he support the character assigned to him with deserved applause."

The applause for Ole Sand was well-deserved but, nevertheless, the stage still seems empty.

Elementary School Principals

In war, hot or cold; in peace, real or contrived, the elementary school principals do every day an indispensable job marked by inconspicuous gallantry.

No position in the school system is more deeply rewarding or less completely rewarded.

Guardian of the pursuit of happiness for the smallest of our vocal citizens; ambassador extra-ordinary (but far from pleni-potentiary) to parents and grandparents, aunts and uncles; professional leader of the most important teachers in the entire range of schooling; architect of the educational foundations without which the rest of the structure of schooling is insecure and incomplete; often unhonored but never without honor—the elementary school principal holds the anchor-position in education's eternal tug-of-war against ignorance and apathy.

Every state should recognize the crucial importance of this post by awarding a special certificate for those who are qualified to hold it.

When the recording angel makes his final report of distinguished services, a substantial part of the *cum laude* list will certainly be devoted to this great group of public servants.

First-Grade Teachers

A first-grade teacher is a young woman (nearly all first-grade teachers are women and all of them are young whatever the calendar says) who can enter a noisy classroom on some enchanted September morning with 30 or more assorted children, stay with them all day, *and survive*.

More: a first-grade teacher can, day by day, hold these children to tasks that are difficult for them, yet allow them to remain children, and come to the end of the school year more loving and beloved than when it started.

A first-grade teacher distributes the little books and gives daily practice in the difficult skill of reading. That miracle is the basis of all books, magazines, and newspapers, of all literature, literacy, and libraries.

A first-grade teacher receives frogs, insects, colored stones, leaves, flowers, and other samples of field and stream and lays the basis for scientific inquiry and understanding of nature.

A first-grade teacher says, "Whose turn is it to clean the blackboard? Do we need a committee to keep our classroom neat?" With such questions the spirit of self-government begins. And all the statutes and legislatures and courts and public authorities stem from such instruction.

This teacher, although 90% of the boys and 60% of the girls will stoutly deny it, is their true and trusted friend, their ally, their betterselves, the source of wisdom, the arbiter of disputes—Minerva with the agate lamp of learning flickering fitfully in one hand and a box of Kleenex at the ready in the other.

The Village Superintendent

In thousands of villages across America an unsung hero plugs ahead with his job. Sometimes "he" is "she." In either case, the title is Superintendent of Schools. There are no office hours—and sometimes no office.

When and if a new school is required the superintendent is largely responsible for the design, the planning (if any), and supervising the contractors. The structure will cost a great deal of money relative to the resources of the small community. It will determine the outward form, and some of the inner substance, of education in that community for the next half-century. If anyone of consequence is not satisfied with the new building, the superintendent might as well start packing. The tradition of the rural superintendent is "build and get fired."

When a school bus driver is ill, the superintendent must find a substitute or drive the route himself. If a teacher resigns in mid-term, the superintendent must take the class while a replacement is sought. The superintendent is purchasing agent, principal, building supervisor, attendance officer, public relations chief, and liaison agent with all the varied elements of the community. When a heavy snow falls, the superintendent decides whether to close the schools and is denounced by about 50% of the community in either case.

His/her personal life is open to public inspection and curiosity. The superintendents hold the school systems together and drive them forward. They rarely win regional or national distinction, but they deserve the eternal gratitude of every citizen.

Most of the time he/she enjoys the job.

School Board Members

The local school board member is not a vanishing species, although sometimes an endangered one. The numbers have declined rapidly in the past few decades because of the consolidation of rural school districts.

Someone should say an unabashedly kind word for these important but harried men and women. To be one of the nation's good school board members should be a civic distinction and a cause of honest pride. They do not serve for personal gain. They rarely use their office as a stepping stone to political advancement or to distribute personal favors or appoint friends to easy jobs. Their leisure is sacrificed to long, long meetings. Their peace of mind is vexed by the necessity of making difficult decisions on emotion-packed issues.

Public denunciation, often cruel and vindictive, is the penalty for error of judgment, real or imagined. Public apathy is often their only evidence that the schools are doing well. Their public responsibilities not only invade their homes but frequently call for sacrifices in their business or professional lives. They receive their full quota of disagreeable letters and telephone calls.

They can take all this in stride because they know that the future of the country depends heavily on the institutions they control.

For the unselfish public service of the local school board member, no adequate payment is possible. So we let most of them go right on working for us for nothing.

Teachers of Handicapped Children

For the routine miracles of teachers in general, there are never adequate words of gratitude. However, for one special group of teachers, those who work with handicapped children, satisfactions come only in the accomplishments of their pupils rather than in their words of appreciation.

Youth never finds it easy to say "thank you," and handicapped children usually have less than average ability to express their feelings.

Let me, therefore, be their unofficial spokesman.

For those who are silenced by defects of speech; for the hyperkinetic; for those whose minds grope in perpetual twilight; for those who see faces but hear no voice; for those who hear but see not; for those who lean too heavily on their teacher and those who shrink away from the teacher's helping hand; for the unstable, the autistic, the endlessly enraged; for the gallant brigades of the wheel-chair, the crutch, and the iron brace; for those with sharp minds in twisted bodies; for those with good muscles and feeble minds: for the unloved, neglected, and rejected; for the indicted delinquent; for the hunted and the haunted; for those grown too tough too soon; for all of those inarticulate ones let me say to each of their teachers, "We all thank you."

The Top Brass

Most of us take public schools for granted, much too much for granted.

We might value the schools more fairly, despite their confessed defects, if we could imagine life after the school doors shut forever. The bookstores would close; it would be useless to print newspapers; the manuals on the operation and repair of our mechanical servants would be even less intelligible than they are at present; epidemics would rage unchecked; elections would lose the last of their significance; skilled workers would be even more maddeningly scarce than they are now; music and the arts would disappear; life would soon become "poor, nasty, brutish, and short."

Managing the indispensable institution of modern civilization is a small group of people called school administrators. They receive up to seven years of formal training for this professional responsibility. Their experience in both teaching and management provides the bridge between community needs and the possibilities of universal education. Their burdens are remorseless, their tenure of office fragile, their monetary rewards modest, their hours of work unceasing, and their influence on the present and future well-being of this nation immeasurable.

In our great cities it is a wonder that anyone is willing to try the job at all.

Clinical Notes

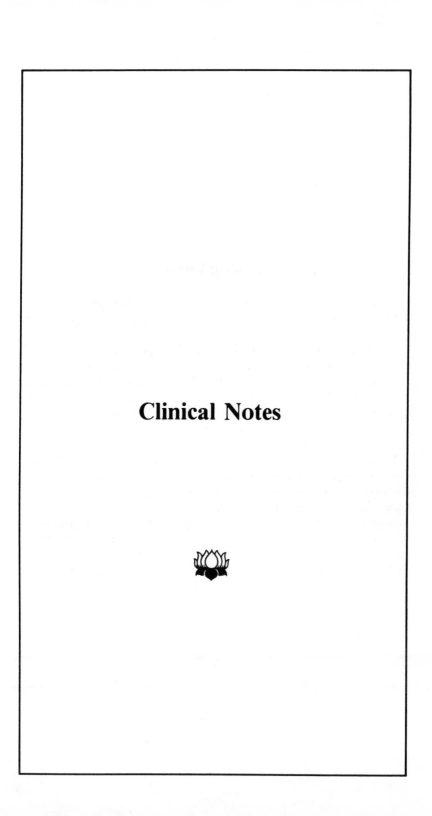

Aristophobia

An aristophobe is a person who displays an irrational fear and hatred of excellence. The fear is clearly visible; the hatred is often hidden but real.

The word "elite" has been withdrawn from polite usage these days. "Elitism" has become a pejorative term. Thus grades and examinations of all kinds are minimized. An aversion arises toward any procedure that compares one person with another; even comparison of the same person's current accomplishments with those of previous years is approached with distaste and apprehension. These viewpoints are all part of the aristophobic syndrome.

Unequal abilities and consequent unequal levels of achievement are facts of life that cannot be rationally ignored. The recognition of competence and merit is far better than recognition of status due to ancestry, color, creed, or economic status.

Inadequate attention to the needs of gifted children, as well as half-hearted motivation to excel, are serious educational disorders. Widespread infection by aristophobia leads to a doubtful prognosis for the well-being of a society and of the individuals who compose it.

Neophilia

A neophile is a patient who irrationally loves what is new—or what is believed to be novel. At its worst the disease exalts novelty into a cult. The neophiliac earnestly believes that schools and other social institutions are invariably better after they change. The votaries of innovation regard the purpose of education as making people "excited" rather than making them wise or (more modestly) informed.

From this basic disorder flows a series of other illusions. Every proposed change becomes at once better than what presently exists. The typical neophile attacks current school practices with crude caricatures, thus creating a straw monster that can be kicked around for the rest of the speech or article. This, in turn, leads to the declaration that the teachers now at work are too lazy, too selfish, too ritual-ridden to change with the changing needs of the times. The neophiles solemnly declare that schools are irrelevant, train for obsolescence, have not changed for 50 years, fail to develop intelligence, are based on fear, punish creativity, and destroy self-reliance. From these "prison-like" schools, children must be "liberated." Indeed, according to neophiles, as things stand, children are being driven to heroin addiction because their schools are so boring.

This list of indictments was not invented; all were found in an afternoon's reading of the current journals of education.

Neophiles are not always in error. It is as irresponsible to declare that whatever is, is right, as it is to cry that all change is an improvement. Tested innovations should be encouraged. Many of the changes wrought by progressive education *were* improvements.

Still many teachers would rather be proven right than be called progressive. There can be too much aimless novelty, too much, even of a good thing.

Resolutionary Paralysis

This malady is sudden in its attack and highly contagious. It may most readily be observed at conventions and other large deliberative meetings.

The onset is typically preceded by several orators who expound the urgent need for action, the perils of delay, and the vast importance of the pending resolution. At a critical point in this process, the delegates begin to strike the palms of their hands together in a steady rhythm. There may be outcries of approval. Sometimes all the sufferers rise together while the peculiar palm-smiting continues at an accelerated pace. This symptom is called a "standing ovation."

After these exertions a vote is taken amid enthusiastic shouts of encouragement. Almost instantly resolutionary paralysis strikes with full force. The victims become convinced that passing the resolution will solve the problems confronting them and that no further effort by anyone is required.

The only known treatment is the injection of a large spine-stiffening dose of personal responsibility. This is a difficult treatment to apply since no rational explanation of further action beyond the resolution is welcomed by the patients.

Even if thus treated, other complications may present themselves. Selective deafness prevents the victims from hearing any discussion of practical ways and means to achieve the goals set forth in the resolution. Infectious lethargy may also reach epidemic dimensions and thus make it very difficult to dispel the usual hallucinations of automatic and effortless success.

Inflationary Palpitation

This puzzling disease sometimes produces hysterical blindness. The symptoms are most readily observed among members of legislative bodies and other governmental officials.

The palpitations of terror may occur when any public expenditure is mentioned, but it is expenditures *for schools* which bring forth the really critical and convulsive aspects of the malady. Most patients with inflationary palpitation react only moderately, if at all, to proposed public expenditures for farmers, roads, veterans, defense, unemployment and other public concerns. These proposals, for reasons not clearly understood, do not give rise to the classic symptoms of inflationary palpitation. It is the suggestion of public expenditures *for schools* that instantly produces the rapid pulse, the clenched teeth, and the clammy hands of advanced inflationary palpitation.

There is, unfortunately, no known treatment. A few patients appear able to outgrow the disease, but in many cases it becomes more violent with the approach of middle age. The disease may be of genetic origin, but probably it should be considered an occupational hazard associated in some manner with the possession of legislative authority.

Adolescent Adulation or AA

A dolescent adulation is a recently recognized disorder in which adults cater to youthful whims. A conference without "youth representation" is regarded as adult tyranny. As a rule the opinions of youth are awaited avidly and received with beaming satisfaction. Their words, no matter how confused or banal, are applauded as if they were the most profound aphorisms ever uttered. The inexperienced are urged to define what is "relevant" not only to their present inclinations but also to their unknown future needs. The young are urged to define relevance not only for their own as yet unattained maturity, but also for those of us who, to put it kindly, are already mature.

Adults suffering from AA believe that only the young can perceive the imperfections of our society and that only the young can prescribe the remedies for the ancient frailties. How did the human race survive thus far without the kindly and sagacious morality of the current generation of youth?

Acquiescence to the current caprices of youth is accompanied by an effort to repeal the laws of learning and to regard disciplined effort as a useless vestige of the past. Youthful slang and mannerisms, youthful experiments in dress and lifestyle, formerly treated with adult forbearance as passing fancies, now provide models for sedulous imitation by highly suggestible adults.

AA is probably one of those diseases that are self-curative after they have run their course. If so, it will again be possible to respect children and youth without condoning or reinforcing their errors. The AA failure to correct error, if long and knowingly continued, is a denial of love, a cynical affirmation of adult indifference, and an abdication of mature responsibility.

Exititis

T he etiology of this disorder is clearly sociological. A growing number of retired people who used to be executives in voluntary organizations, business corporations, or government agencies suffer from *exititis*. There is no cure, but recognizing the symptoms enables some patients to feel more comfortable.

An early symptom in the exititis syndrome is *post-prandial somnolence*. This symptom has been observed after a good lunch as many as 10 years before retirement. Coffee helps. Cold coffee, which is usually freely available at public luncheons, is best.

Another symptom observed is *pernicious loquacity* in which the patient's mind is so packed with memories, happy or otherwise, and he wishes so much to protect his successors from their dreadful inexperience, that a single yes-or-no question evokes a 30-minute response. *Pernicious loquacity* may also occur before actual retirement. Some victims are apparently born with it. A closely related symptom is *aggravated retrospection* when every current question recalls events of the distant past.

An entirely different symptom is *multiple committee adhesions.* The retired patient finds himself on a variety of committees. Not, of course, the Committee to Call at the White House or the Committee to Make a Firsthand Study of Social Trends in Tahiti. No; one serves instead on the routine committees which meet on Saturday evenings. After dinner.

One final symptom, *telephonic debilitation*, requires a brief introduction. An executive becomes accustomed to certain patterns of response when telephoning. For example, a call at 2 p.m. to a staff member is answered by a secretary who says, "Mr. Blank is at lunch, a late lunch, but I will send messengers to every nearby cafe to find him for you." Failing that, she vows that Mr. Blank will return your call the moment he returns to the office. He does, too—90% of the time, anyway.

When *exititis* sets in the response is different. The first words are, "Oh, it's you!" Then, "How are you today?" with a solicitude that suggests that on your retirement you moved 85% of the remaining distance to your final resting place. When the respondent is reassured that you are strong enough to grasp a telephone and of sound enough mind to conduct a coherent conversation, the reply is offered, "Mr. Blank is out." The hour of his return is unknown. Yes, if one wishes, a note will be placed on his desk. Mr. Blank is very busy today but perhaps he can call back Monday—though by then he will be preparing to attend the regional meeting in Honolulu.

With retirement the ravages of *telephonic debilitation* have only begun. The day comes when the patient telephones his former office and is answered by someone unknown—and who has never heard of him, either. The patient is asked, "What organization are you with?" When he replies "none," there is a quick gasp and a long silence, broken at last by a puzzled request for the caller's name. When that request is met there is one more question: "How do you spell it?"

Telephonic debilitation has now run its full course. The patient should have rest and ample fluids. His name should also be dropped from mailing lists lest news of current staff activity elevate his blood pressure dangerously.

Teachers and Teaching

The Mirror Image

In the end the public will take teachers at their own estimate.

If teachers show concern only for the little space within the four walls of a classroom, the public will believe that teachers belong only in the classroom.

If teachers are satisfied with meager preparation and mediocre performance for themselves and their colleagues, the public will conclude that such teachers are good enough.

If teachers are content with small compensation, the public will consider that their work is not worth much.

If teachers present the spectacle of a divided and quarrelsome profession, the public will think that teachers lack common loyalties and purposes.

If teachers fail to ask each other for great efforts in great causes, the public will perceive that their cause is petty and their devotion small.

When teachers broaden their horizons, insist on fair treatment, improve their skills, scorn the dishonest and incompetent among their number, discover unity in purpose and action, the profession will receive public respect by earning it.

As the mirror is always faithful to that which stands before it, so will be the public's estimate of teachers to teachers' estimate of themselves.

General Education For Teachers

A good general education is needed by every teacher. I make no exception for the teachers of little children. The youngest children learn much from the intellectual and cultural background of their adult companions. Growing minds raise questions that range far beyond the textbook—"questions that would cross a rabbi's eyes," as Tevye says in *Fiddler on the Roof.*

General education helps any teacher to feel at home in his world and in his times, with a sense of confident readiness to deal with a wide range of topics. No teacher whose mind is shackled to the textbook in one subject can do well at any school level. Only an education of generous breadth and depth can entitle a teacher to the necessary respect of pupils, parents, colleagues, and the adult community as a whole.

Quarrelsome differences used to exist on this point between "scholars" and "educators," so called. Such differences are diminishing. The scholars no longer insist that mastery of subject matter is the only requisite for a competent teacher. The more distinguished the scholars, I have observed, the more ready they are to allow such concessions. Meanwhile, fewer teachers continue to denigrate scholarship. Most important, leaders in teacher education welcome the conclusion that a good general education is an important ingredient in preparing for the teaching service.

Distinctive or Diluted?

Every teacher should be an expert in some subject of instruction. This generalization is most obvious in the secondary schools and colleges where fields of knowledge are usually taught separately. However, I would not exclude elementary school teachers. True, one need not know differential calculus in order to teach how to multiply fractions. Yet a teacher who does not perceive in beginning studies the implications for more advanced studies is too closely bound by the routine memories of his own childhood. The pursuit of further knowledge is, for teachers, an important aspect of the pursuit of happiness.

Certification requirements for high school teachers usually require that about one-seventh of the time en route to the baccalaureate be devoted to courses in education as a subject of study. For elementary school teachers the comparable proportion is about one-fifth.

Almost all public appraisal of teacher preparation has been concentrated on these small fractions. Surely we should consider with at least equal concern the other six-sevenths or four-fifths of the total.

For example, I once met a professor of Elizabethan literature who required his graduate students to count the feminine endings of the lines in each of Shakespeare's plays. The professor was testing a theory that the proportion of such lines was a clue to the age of the playwright. I never learned—or have since forgotten—whether or not this ingenious hypothesis was confirmed by our investigations. That was all long ago and far away and it did not help me to teach English composition in junior high school.

The point is that graduate specialization is not in itself a guarantee of quality teaching. Prospective teachers do not require graduate preparation that is made easy, but rather preparation that is relevant to their work, not diluted preparation but distinctive preparation.

Know-How and Know-Why

A lawyer needs a broad education and a detailed knowledge of legal principles. But I also want my lawyer to know courtroom procedures, when and where to file a brief, and how to examine hostile witnesses.

A physician needs a broad education and a detailed knowledge of medicine and anatomy. But I also want my doctor to know anesthesia, the use of a scalpel, how to read blood-pressure, and use a stethoscope.

So, also, with teachers. The skills of teaching cannot be properly learned by casual observation. It has been erroneously said that teaching skill can be intuitively acquired on the job by applying common sense to the teacher's memory of his own experience as a student. If so, a passenger who has logged a hundred thousand miles in the cabin is qualified to change places with the navigator in the cockpit.

An illustration: Suppose a child is not learning to read well. There are a dozen possible reasons for this situation. A person with a liberal arts degree *cum laude* and a Ph.D. in English literature can only guess at the cause of the difficulty. Both know-how and know-why are required to design and conduct a program to ameliorate the problem.

It is silly to argue for techniques without scholarship and without general education. A more reasoned analysis will lead to the conclusion that education, like other professions, needs all three.

The Well-Known Teacher

H enry Van Dyke wrote eloquently about "The Unknown Teacher." My theme, however, is the well-known teacher who has attracted national attention for excellent work. The "Golden Key" awards, the "Teacher of the Year" selections provide a series of examples. I have studied the traits of these nationally-recognized teachers and would like to share what I found out.

First, these successful and respected teachers all had close and extensive contacts with their communities. They visit community institutions. They take part in local civic activities. They are not "two-by-four" teachers enclosed in the two covers of a textbook and the four walls of a schoolroom. They function in the tradition of the great teachers who met their pupils in the bustling market place of ancient Athens.

Second, these distinguished teachers are dedicated to their calling. They do not sneer at their colleagues or belittle themselves. They are proud to teach. Concerning one of them a student wrote, "I wish his class could last *two* hours." Not very eloquent words, perhaps, but from such a source, a profound tribute.

Third, superior teachers work hard and require the same of their students. They refuse to regard teaching as just another job. They did not become teachers to serve as robots on some dreary educational assembly line for a good hourly union wage.

Finally, outstanding teachers admire their students. One of these teachers was asked by a visitor whether he had any gifted children in his class. "Madam," he bristled, "*every* student in my class is gifted." Another teacher looks over each entering class with proud anticipation. Each year she says, "This class is the best I *ever* had"—and means it.

Community contacts, dedication, hard work, and admiration for their students—these are four hallmarks of teachers who are recognized as unusually successful.

The Vanishing Distinction

I n many nations, elementary education is intended for everyone, but secondary education is for a select group. The effort to provide secondary education to all, or very nearly all, of our youth was a unique American experiment and remains only a tentative possibility in most of the rest of the world.

The friendly cooperation and commonality of basic purpose that unite elementary and secondary education in America are unknown in many countries where the two levels of education are almost separate enterprises.

Even the word for teacher may be different at the two levels. The French secondary school teacher is usually a *professeur,* whilst the teacher in an elementary school is an *instituteur.* The *professeur* instructs *étudiants,* or students; the classes of the *instituteur* are composed of *élèves,* or pupils. The two groups of teachers are rarely regarded as colleagues; they belong to different unions, they are trained in different institutions, and a social distinction exists between the two.

These differences, deep-rooted as they are, have been eroded in recent years as various school reforms and experiments have been tried around the world. Before long the differences will have vanished.

Meanwhile, it is worth remembering that this country pioneered the concept of one education, adapted to individual differences, but open equally to all. This may well be the most important and enduring contribution of America to evolving human culture.

Does it seem impossible that the day will ever come when teachers in schools and in colleges will feel and act like colleagues in the same profession? It seems like a widely improbable prophecy now, but it will happen, and sooner than many people expect.

Moral Values and the Teacher

The public schools are teaching moral values to the nearly 90% of all young Americans who attend them. This teaching is mostly incidental and, for that reason, all the more powerful. It is not, however, being done as well as either the public or the school people would like. Many teachers are not doing as good a job as they know how to do. Large classes, crowded buildings, community apathy, and social and familial forces sometimes work against the best efforts of the schools.

We now live in an era when there is confusion among Americans about the values that ought to be taught. Our grandparents seem to have generally assumed that the more people knew the better they would behave. That illusion has been shattered by wars, depressions, barbaric behavior by "civilized" people, recurrent government scandals, and social disasters in the wake of scientific triumphs.

Many adults, including teachers, are now uncertain about moral issues on which their ancestors entertained no possible shadow of doubt. Now, like the monarch in *The King and I*, we face moral issues with the reluctant admission that "It is a puzzlement."

Doubts about values are compounded by other uncertainties. Some critics declare that the schools neglect character education. What these critics really mean, at heart, is that the schools fail because they do not teach religion. Each critic, of course, means *his* religion, although collectively the critics find it convenient to ignore the substantial and sometimes bitter sectarian differences that exist.

On the whole, however, the schools have maintained more of the nation's idealism than has society at large. Cynical teachers are still a minority, although perhaps a growing one. Most teachers still possess strong moral convictions. Without such sustenance they could hardly survive as teachers.

Still a Matter of Opinion

A little knowledge is a dangerous thing. Several studies have shown that, on the usual types of pencil-and-paper tests, large classes produce as good scores as smaller classes.

Almost all the important questions, however, remain unanswered: the effect of large classes on health; their effect on the mental stability of the teachers; the effect of a large class on a shy or timid child; on the rowdy, the bully, the precocious. What is the effect of the physical size of the classroom on different size enrollments? Do teachers of small classes know their students better than those of large classes? If so, how do teachers use this knowledge? What other factors tend to increase the teachers' understanding of individual pupils? Do parents as a rule prefer large or small classes, or don't they care? If they prefer small classes, what do they expect their children to gain from the preferred environment?

The simple conclusion that class size doesn't matter because standard test scores are unaffected is like describing a continent when only part of the coast line has been viewed.

Many studies of class size confused that variable with the total responsibility of the teacher. How do the results of four classes of 30 pupils each compare with those of two classes of 60 pupils? Or eight classes of 15 pupils?

The public, with calm disregard for the issues involved, makes three demands on the schools: teach more pupils, teach them better, do it all cheaper. The teacher's load is a very real problem, but the man in the street still thinks teaching is a "soft" job.

In 1799, when George Washington was seeking a good school for his nephew, he wrote to his agent in Philadelphia, "I lay it down as a maxim that if the number of pupils is too great for the tutors, justice cannot be done. . . . What the due proportion is, beyond which it ought not to be permitted to go, is in some measure a matter of opinion."

It still is.

Start Early

Controversy about the nature of intelligence has given rise to a vast and bewildering literature. No conclusions can yet claim universal endorsement, but a few points do approach the level of fairly widespread agreement. Here are a few of the generally accepted conclusions:

Intelligence is not completely fixed at birth. It is to some extent subject to nurture and experience, especially so during the early years.

Mental processes and habits of thought established early in life exert long-range effects, for good or ill, on lifelong intellectual activity.

Loss of development during the first years of life cannot be fully recovered at subsequent periods.

The unescapable conclusion from these general observations is the importance of the early years of learning. Men and women who are concerned with the most advanced levels of scholarship and scientific research ought to show more concern than they now typically exhibit for home life, nursery schools, kindergartens, and primary education.

The college professor who seeks to advance scholarship by concentrating his attention on the collegiate preparation given in the secondary schools is calling for the fire department after the conflagration has nearly burned itself out.

School: Slow Down

In the early years of this century junior high schools were established to achieve "economy of time." The new school, it was said, would permit youth to begin employment at an earlier age.

We have hastened the tempo of life until we seem to be becoming a nation of neurotics and dyspeptics. Ulcers and nerves jangle us all the days of our adult lives. We have accelerated the pace of industry, commerce, transportation, communication, marriage, and divorce. Must we speed up the children, too?

In the primary grades we have added an enriching mixture of "activities" and "projects" to the minimal basics of education required in the nineteenth century. And we are trying to shove the children through the entire whirl in less time than ever. No genuine needs of society require or justify this remorseless preoccupation with swift results.

The junior high or middle school, strategically located in the midsection of the public school ladder, is in a good position to moderate the speed-up. Although its original mission was greater velocity, perhaps in this new day, the junior high could help to calm things down.

It would not be the first social institution to be created for one purpose and then converted to another.

The street signs read "School: Slow Down." We should use some of the same warnings inside the schools and in the offices of educational policy-makers.

The number of years the average person spends in school is steadily increasing. Nevertheless, the speed-up and the stretch-out are still common in school programs. Why not let some of the leeway be used to meet the demands of the human organism for rest, refreshment, and variety? What, after all, is the hurry?

Mine Eyes Have Seen

O nce, at a teacher's meeting, we were entertained by a junior high school chorus of about 50 girls. They faced the audience in three orderly rows on risers across the stage.

One of the girls in the front row clung to the hand of her neighbor. She was black and she was blind. Since she could not see the conductor she received her cues to sing and to be silent from the pressure of her neighbor's hand. I wondered how well this arrangement would work.

I soon found out, for their opening number was "The Battle Hymn of the Republic." That blind girl sang the opening verse as a solo. Her voice rang out clearly, as she sang the words, "Mine eyes have *seen* the glory. . . ."

I thought then about the ideal of education for all. I thought that without this ideal, the very best in life that girl could have hoped for would have been a life of fear and frustration in some dark quiet corner. I asked myself what it was worth to teach this girl to read with her fingertips and to sing and to smile. And I knew that no amount of money in all the world would provide a sensible answer to that inane question.

Steadily on the Whole System

I n 1821 Thomas Jefferson, discussing the future of education in Virginia wrote: "Let us keep our eyes steadily on the whole system." Precisely—let us see education steadily and see it whole.

It might help if we desisted from referring so often to the "levels" of education. The elementary schools, the high schools, and the colleges each have essential roles. But American education is not a three-layer cake with a thin icing of adult education on top. We might better picture it as a complex intermeshed mechanism in which no part can run properly unless all parts move together.

A unified approach to the financing of education would also help. It is difficult enough to get money for education; we can ill afford competitive and uncoordinated pleas for funds from each part of the school system.

In social institutions, as in engines, the enemy of efficiency is friction. For this there are two remedies. One of them is oil or lubrication in the form of mutual respect and conciliatory words. How lucky we are that the public does not believe all the harsh things educators say about each other!

The second way to reduce friction is to redesign the points of contact. This requires careful review of curricula based on both the shared and the unique responsibilities of schools and colleges.

We would greatly improve American education if all teachers would agree that from bib-and-tucker to cap-and-gown, they are engaged in a common vocation. "All waste," said John Dewey, "is due to isolation. Organization is nothing but getting things into connection." If a supposedly impractical philosopher can see and say that, why can't practical people act upon it?

When teachers and professors discover that they are engaged in the same occupation, they will enhance the quality of the whole system. We need to end the mistrust, and what is worse, the indifference with which too many teachers now regard each other.

Episodes in the History

of Education

Ye Ould Deluder

Over 330 years ago, on November 11, 1647, to be exact, the General Court (or legislature) of the Massachusetts Bay Colony enacted the most important single piece of school legislation in the history of America, perhaps the most important in the history of organized education anywhere.

The law began with the now-famous words, "It being one chief project of ye ould Deluder, Satan, to keep man from the knowledge of ye Scriptures. . ." After this preamble, the law ordered every town with 50 households to appoint at once a teacher of reading and writing and to provide his wages. Every town with 100 or more households was directed to provide also a grammar school to prepare youths for Harvard.

There was no precedent for such a law. In its view of the power of the state, the law was as daring as any document in American history. The state required local communities to provide schools and assessed penalties for failure to obey. It established, in effect, that children must be educated, not chiefly to advance the welfare of the individual child but rather because society as a whole suffers if ignorance prevails. For all its old fashioned style, the "Ould Deluder" statute was a landmark of lasting importance.

Though the colonists who wrote the law are dust these many years and their names forgotten, the principles on which they acted have broadened down through the decades and the centuries. They provided the basis for the vast body of law on public education, which now supports and regulates the educational system of the United States.

"To Redeem the Poor and Distressed"

In 1797 in the sweltering heat of Madras, Dr. Andrew Bell had a school for orphans. In the British colonies, as in the mother country, individual instruction was then the standard procedure. But Dr. Bell had so many pupils that one-to-one teaching was impossible. Necessity gave birth to invention. Dr. Bell introduced a plan he called "mutual instruction," organized around a system of pupil-teachers.

At about the same time an English schoolmaster named Joseph Lancaster, having a large school and being too poor to employ additional teachers, organized a corps of student monitors. The idea spread across the Atlantic via New York City to other U.S. centers. In 1826 Maryland organized Lancastrian schools on a statewide basis.

The management of up to 1000 pupils in one large hall was undoubtedly an impressive sight. It required a mechanized course of study, the liberal use of student teachers, an elaborate system of bells and signals, and robots for pupils. The teacher taught the monitors; each of these in turn passed the flickering flame of learning on to a small group of younger pupils. The teacher had only to organize, to reward, and to punish; the system did the rest.

DeWitt Clinton, governor of New York and an ardent champion of free public schools, wrote of the new system in lyrical words:

> Boys in our school have been taught to read and write in two months, who did not before know the alphabet. . . . When I contemplate the habits of order which it forms, the spirit of emulation which it excites, . . . the purity of morals which it inculcates, . . . and when I perceive one great Assembly of 1000 children, marching with unexampled rapidity and with perfect discipline to the goal of knowledge, I confess that I recognize in Lancaster the benefactor of the human race . . . a blessing from Heaven to redeem the poor and distressed.

In 1815 Dr. Bell visited Pestalozzi at Yverdon. On leaving, Dr. Bell predicted, "In another 12 years mutual instruction will be adopted by the whole world and Pestalozzi's method will be forgotten." Such a gross error of forecast could easily be made by one who thought the main object of education is to *inform* while observing one who knew that the main object is to *develop*.

The Maryland State experiment lasted just two years. Thus one more plan for operating schools without the annoying expense of teachers passed into history's wastebin.

Lincoln and Buchanan

When Congress passed the first bill to provide a small federal subsidy to the land-grant colleges in 1859, President Buchanan vetoed the measure. Most Americans have probably forgotten that there was a president named Buchanan. His veto was one of the few things he did to make himself remembered.

In his veto message, the President explained that this legislation was an entering wedge, that federal control of these colleges would follow federal funds as surely as night follows day, that the states would reduce their own efforts in higher education and that the foundations of the Republic would begin to crumble on the day that federal funds were spent for education in the states.

Two years later, another president whose name will not be forgotten came to the White House. The least informed citizen remembers the name of Abraham Lincoln. He signed the bill into law. Nothing bad has happened because he did so. The states still control their own systems of higher education. Despite Buchanan's fears that the states would diminish their own efforts to finance education if the federal government gave them a hand, the states instead immensely magnified their efforts.

The land-grant colleges, by conservative estimates, must have added to the wealth of the nation a thousand dollars for every dollar supplied by the federal government. Over a century later their instruction, research, and community services continue to enrich the nation.

Strikes and State Responsibility

It is sometimes forgotten that a local board of education is the agent not only of the local community, but also of the state in which it is located and by which it has been created.

In 1897 in Watervliet, New York, the local school board was unable to secure a majority vote that would permit it to employ the school staff. After waiting a few weeks for the local board to reconcile its differences, and having waited in vain, the New York State Commissioner of Education directed one of his aides to proceed to Watervliet, assume the duties of acting school superintendent, employ the necessary personnel, and operate the public schools.

Certain taxpayers of Watervliet asked the state supreme court for an injunction to restrain the state commissioner. The court denied the request, declaring that the local board had failed to perform its duty to open the schools. The reasons for this failure, said the court, are of little consequence, but to deprive a city of public school services is a matter of great moment. The school system is an institution of the state, said the court, and the people of the entire state have a legitimate interest in the matter.

Is it now time to ask whether the failure to open public schools because the local school board and the teachers' organization cannot agree on salaries and conditions of employment is a denial of educational opportunity calling for state intervention? Lawyers could and would argue long on this question but the Watervliet decision suggests an affirmative answer.

Gone Are the Days

Only 50 years ago there were 150,000 one-teacher schools. The typical school for rural children was a frame structure valued at $1,000, site and furniture included.

The typical rural school was directed by the tiniest cell in the body politic—a local school board of three persons elected for three-year terms. Only one member in 20 was a woman. Practically all of the men were farmers. This board had legal power to make contracts, buy and sell property, levy taxes, buy supplies, admit and suspend pupils, and appraise their work.

The board had one employee—usually a young woman teacher on a one-year contract. She administered rewards and punishments; cared for the children in case of bad weather, accidents, or sudden illness; inspected the water supply; managed entertainments to raise money for school supplies; kept the building clean; and stoked the school stove as weather required. She also taught all the subjects in each of the eight grades. For these services she was paid $750 per year.

She boarded in a home near the school where the chances were no better than two out of three that she had a room of her own.

Her school had 20 pupils with an average age of about 12. The school year was 160 days, five hours and five minutes per day. Each of the 30 classes she taught took 10 to 15 minutes of her time. She devoted one-third of the total time to the 3R's, eight percent to language, six percent each to geography and spelling, and four percent each to physical training and history. She also scheduled classes in penmanship, nature study, science, music, and health.

Rural school children almost invariably scored below urban children on comparable tests. This statistic was well-known but regarded as inevitable.

These inadequate conditions nevertheless required substantial financial sacrifice. Taxes claimed about one-third of the farmer's net revenue and about half of his taxes were devoted to the school.

Lest we forget, that is the way it was.

The Earthquake

The depression of the 1930s hit the schools like a devastating earthquake. The most lasting result of the tremor was not the instant damage but rather the revelation of weak spots, which geologists would call faults, in the very structure of public school finance.

It is imprecise to say that the faults were uncovered by the catastrophe. Long before the first shocks of the depression, it was well-known that the system of financing schools was, in most states, archaic, inadequate, and shockingly inequitable. Moreover, a cultivated hysteria about taxation had led many citizens to conclude that public expenditures were inherently evil.

A tax-strike psychology, plus a depression, plus an inefficient public revenue system combined to produce an extensive emergency in education.

It would be nice to report that these old faults have now been repaired. There were indeed some improvements but none of the changes was extensive enough to protect the nation from a re-run in the Seventies of the calamities of the Thirties.

As an educational event, the Great Depression was a failure. We didn't learn enough, so now we may have to repeat the course.

Charts Revisited

Fifty years ago students of school administration learned the relationships in a school system by drawing charts. At the top of the page we drew a small rectangle representing "The Voters." These voters elected about seven of the most virtuous and sagacious of their fellow citizens to "The School Board." It was installed in a larger rectangle dangling just below that of "The Voters." In this choice little group no self-promoters, axe-grinders, hate-mongers, or ex-teachers were allowed.

The school board, following procedures fully detailed in our textbooks, selected "The Superintendent of Schools." He (for he it almost invariably was) occupied the largest rectangle, right in the middle of the page. Below him, hung the rectangles for his professional staff— "The Assistant Superintendents in Charge of This and That," then "The School Principals" in stately array, then the well-ordered rank and file of "The Classroom Teachers." Below them, clinging precariously to the bottom edge of the page came "The Pupils."

It was an enchanting chart, as efficient as a packing plant. No voter could get to the schools except through the school board. No teacher could get to the school board except through the superintendent. We knew of course that superintendents could have their terms terminated by means other than death or retirement. We even read in some jaundiced newspapers that some school board members were rascals and that not all of them were intellectually gifted.

Still, in our bright lexicons, there was no such word as "compromise." Our charts showed how things ought to be, and would be, too, when we took our places in those big central rectangles. Meanwhile, with all the patience and modesty of youth, we let the schools muddle along.

> "Bliss was it then to be alive,
> And to be young was very Heaven."

Ethics for the Brass

In view of the current interest in ethical (and even more in unethical) conduct in the Congress, it is useful to recall that a quarter-century ago the Louisiana School Board Association made news by proclaiming a code of ethics for its members. The code included:

Freedom from subservience to political party interests
Refusal to seek special privilege or private gain
Responsibility to provide educational opportunity for all
Recognition of the executive role of the school superintendent
No pressure for the employment of friends or relations
Not committing the board prior to action by the board
Acceptance of decisions by the board majority
Sincere effort to keep informed about school issues
No public criticism of school personnel
Economy and efficiency in management of public expenditure
Attendance at school board meetings with an open mind
Full compliance with the school laws of the state

What happened to this code after it was promulgated I do not know, but it is safe to assume that maximum interest in ethics was displayed at the time the code was drafted and issued.

Cynics will say that those who approve such a code do not need one, while for those who will not abide by the code, its acceptance is hypocrisy. Yet, a public commitment to vows of high principle is worthy of praise. The code, at the very least, makes it clear that those who serve the public have agreed on what constitutes upright and responsible conduct.

The Next Fifty Years

Prophesy is always a safer exercise if it considers the remote future. It is easier to predict the next century than to guess what will happen tomorrow morning. Long-range forecasts protect one from being accountable for those same forecasts.

However, back in 1950 I was coaxed into a prediction for the next 50 years. Now that more than half that period has elapsed, I can review my score as a forecaster. I said:

1. "The struggle between the Soviet and non-Soviet worlds will continue . . . punctuated by brief periods of relative serenity." *Check.*

2. "The public will be apprehensive lest alien philosophies gain a foothold in our schools." *Check.*

3. "National unity will be a major concern." *Check.*

4. Large expenditures "to aid potential allies and for national defense will make school finance increasingly difficult." *Double check.*

5. "Annual per capita production will increase to about $2500 per year." *That was a major error. By 1975 the figure was over $6000 and rising. I failed to allow for inflation and the increased gainful employment of women.*

6. "The public will use part of our increased production to provide more generously for the health and education of our youth." *Excessive youthful optimism.*

7. "Public interest in education will remain about the same as before." *Check.*

8. "The public will put its foot down on some of the undesirable effects of school and college athletics." *Wrong, so far; but I let the prediction stand for the year 2000.*

9 "Unless social change keeps closer to technological change, many dreadful social upheavals will result." *Check.*

10. "Citizens will continue to prize self-reliance, poise, honesty, industry, and consideration for others." *Check.*

That is the record. Whether it compares favorably with Jeremiah, Nostradamus, and Jean Dixon is a question for others to decide.

What Happened to Teaching?

In the decades beginning about 1955 these changes occurred in the teaching corps of the United States:

1. It grew younger. The average age of all teachers fell from 41 to 33 in the 15 years before 1976.
2. It was better educated. The typical teacher without a degree became a teacher with a four-year college degree, plus some graduate study. By 1976 some 37% had a master's degree or six years of college study.
3. The proportion of men in teaching rose steadily, not only in the high schools but also at the elementary school level.

These and other statistical changes produced some new characteristics in the teaching profession which, in turn, profoundly modified the public school itself.

By 1965 the teachers had constructed a brighter vision of their careers. Youth would be served. Great expectations arose with youthful idealism. The young men, mostly as heads of new and growing families, had a stronger impulse to seek higher pay. Status also became important. The younger, better educated teachers would no longer accept limitations on their civic and professional rights.

The new teachers had learned to be ambitious. They demanded a greater share in the affluent society; they demanded a chance to apply their increased knowledge to assail the most difficult socio-economic problems of the day.

Above all, the new recruits were impatient. Action now became their watchword. As youth has always done, they questioned the established patterns and values. This generation wanted instant gratification. The teachers in the 1960s reached for power, seized it, and used it not only to improve their own status but to make profound changes in the spirit of the American school. In the 1980s those changes have been codified and consolidated; they are now irreversible.

Cruel and Unusual Punishment

If we despair because of the inequities and cruelties of some aspects of some schools in these days, it is consoling to look back over the past.

Charlotte Bronte in *Jane Eyre*, Charles Dickens in *Nicholas Nickleby*, and many other writers have made us aware of the wretched conditions in English schools of the nineteenth century. These books are fiction but their schoolroom scenes are true to life.

If fiction will not persuade us, we can turn to biography for further evidence. Such a work as Stephan Zweig's life of Honoré de Balzac recounts the vicious school experiences to which the great French novelist was subjected. Sent to a boarding school at the age of seven, the gifted and sensitive boy was subjected to extremes of cruelty and neglect: no holidays, a Spartan discipline, 80 boys in one dirty classroom, miserable food, inadequate clothing, severe and frequent beatings, even the stocks and the pillory for the least inattention or variation from arduous and arbitrary routine. For seven years not one teacher treated the boy as an individual, offered one word or token of kindness, or recognized the Promethean genius yeasting in that youthful mind.

The poorest school in the Western world today is infinitely superior when compared to the common practices of earlier periods of education. The contemplation of education's history may give us hope as well as wisdom.

Good Riddance

G erman education shall be so controlled as to completely eliminate Nazi and militaristic doctrines and to make possible the successful development of democratic ideas.

These words from the 1945 Potsdam Declaration guided the reform that ended one of the most evil perversions of education ever devised. Goodbye to the columns of haggard girls and boys marching stiffly to honor the Fuehrer; goodbye to Aryan racial superiority as part of the required curriculum from age 6 on; goodbye to instruction which had led children to report their parents to the Gestapo; goodbye to the swastika painted on the brows of Jewish children; goodbye to arithmetic books full of problems on long-range bombing; goodbye to kindergarten prayers that thanked Hitler for daily bread; goodbye to artful lies presented as heroic history; goodbye to the Hitler Jugend, the Bund Deutscher Madchen, and all the swarming Nazi sycophants; goodbye to all that.

Teachers from all parts of the world solemnly voted that they would end such malpractice forever and never stand idly by while any nation twists the minds and morality of its innocent children and forbids intellectual freedom. How many teachers today remember? How many would act on the Potsdam Declaration's high resolutions?

The Last Lap

Years ago, H. G. Wells said (and has been quoted and misquoted ever since) that "Civilization is a race between education and catastrophe." That centuries-long race has lately entered a new phase.

On July 16, 1945, on a desert plateau in New Mexico, there occurred an explosive release of atomic energy—the first such event in history. The bomb vaporized a heavy 200-foot steel tower. It emblazoned the surrounding bleakness with a searing radiance equal to that from twenty suns. In Albuquerque, over 200 miles away, a blind girl started and asked her mother what had happened.

What, indeed, had happened? That explosion was the starting gun for the last lap of the race between education and catastrophe. The race is not new. The discovery of ways to release atomic energy does not pose a new problem. It does put a time limit (certain, even if its duration remains unknown) on the solution of a problem as old as human culture itself. To teach the youth of all lands a strong sense of individual moral responsibility and to do it quickly, effectively, and universally is the answer to the awful dangers and breath-taking opportunities that atomic power presents.

There is no other answer. The last lap in Mr. Wells's race is being run right now.

Flights of Fancy

Our Closing Speaker

To be the closing speaker on a long program is a fate of dire portent. There can be only two reasons why the program committee listed you last. They think you are either very good or very bad. If the former, they hope you will send the weary audience home inspired, amused, and glad they stayed—an expectation more apt to produce in the speaker greater anxiety than exhilaration. If the latter, the committee has decided that the many people who will leave before and during your remarks will not miss much.

When you are called to the rostrum as "our closing speaker," you must choose among several strategies, none of which has great allure.

1. If you summarize the observations of the previous speakers, the audience will think they should have walked out after the earlier part of the program and escape the rehash.

2. If you deliver a statement prepared in advance of the meeting, you have brazenly made up your mind before you even heard the opinions of the other speakers.

3. If you launch into a nice mixture of wit and eloquence, you will be justly subject to the criticism that you are out of touch with the serious problems the conference was called to consider.

So, you can't win. The only way is to have a program committee that invites only one speaker to stand up, speak out, and sit down. They should excise from the program the minutes of the previous meeting, the treasurer's report, the introduction of platform guests, and the piano solo by the chairperson's grandchild. That way everyone could start home in less than an hour. The closing speaker would also be the opening speaker and harmony and joy would abound.

But shrimps will learn to whistle ere that gladsome day arrives.

SH!

In 1946, believe it or not, New York City received the annual award of the Noise Abatement Council. The memory of this odd event suggests that it is time to organize a School Noise Abatement Council (SNAC) with the following goals:

First, disconnect and trash-compact most of the bells now used to punctuate the school day. These electric horrors are usually loud enough to loosen the teeth, deform the ears, and curdle the brains of any child or teacher within 100 feet. SNAC will replace these monsters with mellow chimes.

SNAC will also place before a firing squad (rifles equipped with silencers, of course) all persons who buy or sell steel cafeteria chairs that cannot be quietly moved. The sound of 200 steel chairs simultaneously gliding their 800 iron feet across a cement floor is indescribable by polite adjectives. Neither the noise nor the adjectives will promote digestion.

Life imprisonment will be the penalty for any school designer who locates the band practice room next to the class in English poetry or puts the gymnasium within 50 feet of the class in music appreciation.

Finally, double life imprisonment in a boiler factory for those who locate the history and math classrooms right on the main street with its yammering cacophony of passing traffic, while the school's wood and metal shops raise their industrious din on the quiet back residential streets where they disturb and enrage the neighbors.

Other programs will be quietly developed as SNAC grows and prospers. Contributions to SNAC should be sent in folding money only, lest the clink of coins being counted jar the serene silence of SNAC's sound-proofed offices.

Sky-Larking

The event may not be listed in *The Guinness World Book of Records*, but the world's long distance truancy record was set some years ago by a young Arabian prince attending a school in Rhode Island. The missing youngster was found the next day by the royal truant officer at a Paris airport. This is truancy in the grand style. Many American youngsters must have read about His Royal Highness's escapade with profound feelings of inadequacy.

Any lingering doubt as to whether modern technology has had an impact on education should be removed by this event. Now that students have begun using jet aircraft to skip school, it will soon be necessary to equip truant officers with small pursuit planes. Modern school systems will park their search-and-seizure aircraft under the football bleachers. Someone will write a doctoral thesis on the aesthetic and moral values of skipping school by air. Someone else will set up cost standards per retrieval for air truancy. The AASA will appoint a committee to determine under what circumstances school districts should own a plane or lease one.

Someday, no doubt, the Supreme Court, which lately misses no opportunity to advise us all on educational policy, will decide whether a public school plane bound homeward to Seattle with a truant picked up in Tampa may legally stop in Emporia to pick up another truant from St. Joseph's Academy in Spokane.

Thus technology in the service of education continues to pose new issues of educational policy, which must be confronted with courage and compassion.

A Remarkable Visual Aid

A fter many years of research and development, a remarkable visual aid is now being produced. It can be controlled by the learner without the need for constant attention from the teacher. It can present with equal ease current information, historical records, or even imaginative flights into the future.

The device is practically foolproof. It has no moving parts to get out of order. It never needs adjustment or lubrication and requires repairs only after many years of use. It requires no special instruction manual. It needs no wires or electrical connections. It is entirely portable and can be used at home as easily as in school.

It is so inexpensive that each individual student may own one without excessive cost. It is unbreakable under almost all conditions of use. There are no expenses for operation. Replacements, if required, are easily available. It occupies little space and is completely self-contained.

This wonderful visual aid to education has, in fact, been available for many years. At the present time, for a variety of reasons, it is not as widely employed as it used to be. However, it is possible to hope that this convenient aid to learning will eventually be more widely and wisely used. It is called—a Book.

He/She

The liberation of women revealed some serious shortages in the English language. The word "mankind" has to be replaced, albeit imprecisely, by the word "people." We are assaulted by such ungainly nouns as "chairperson" and "spokesperson." Close behind, no doubt, lurk "midshipperson" and "junkperson."

As consciousness increases, we also suffer such ungraceful expressions as he/she, her/him, and his/hers. We desperately need an ambisexual singular personal pronoun. We must invent one. English is a resilient living language and can withstand a great deal of person-handling without serious harm.

I propose that we all use the single word "shim" to avoid the awkward he/she, her/him combinations. Instead of writing of some future President, "He/she will be inaugurated on January 20, 1995," we shall write "Shim will be inaugurated . . . ." In more complex situations, consider such a sentence as "The Professor told each student that shim's term paper must be in shim's office before a final grade will be awarded to shim." Anyone can see how this would simplify speech and allow us to refer to professors and students without discriminatory sex-role stereotypes.

I hope to be known as the inventor of "shim" in the same way as the founder of Father's Day is forever remembered by a grateful nation.

Next project: and/or.

Why?

Many new school buildings are being planned much better than were the buildings they replace. However, opportunity remains for greater innovation and adaptability.

Why should every classroom have the same color scheme? And usually drab-dreary colors at that? Why not let parents, teachers, and children choose from a chart of color schemes?

Why should a teacher's desk be just like the desk of a minor business executive? Who will design a work space for a teacher comparable in compactness, utility, and convenience to that of a dentist's work space?

Why must school cafeterias echo like concatenated bedlams and smell forever of cream-of-tomato soup? Why not build school lunch rooms in a series of sound-proof ventilated alcoves, each seating from 12 to 20 children?

Why must all the trees on a new school site be felled and carried away before construction starts?

Schools are places where people live and learn together. Consultation with the future inhabitants would tend to produce buildings that will, in themselves, teach lessons of beauty, grace, health, order, serenity, efficiency, and respect for individual differences. Why not?

Begin with Me

Once I heard a Chinese philosopher, Dr. Hu Shih, tell an old Chinese legend.

Long ago in a remote region of Cathay, lived an emperor who longed to promote the happiness and prosperity of his people.

One advisor suggested that the emperor invite experts from all over the world to visit his country and develop its resources. Another counselor advised him to build up a strong imperial army. The Lord Chancellor urged the emperor to develop profitable trade between his empire and the rest of the world.

The emperor, bewildered by multiple choices and racked by indecision, knew not what to do. Touring his kingdom in this state of bewilderment and turning over in his mind the various possibilities, he happened to pass by the school he had attended as a boy. In front of the school, so the legend goes, the emperor saw his former teacher now stooped with the passage of years. The emperor commanded his carriage to halt and addressed the ancient pedagogue.

"Distinguished and venerable teacher," he said, "I desire to promote the happiness of my people. I have money to spend for this purpose and much conflicting advice about how to spend it. Tell me, venerable master, where should I start?"

The answer was instant. "Your Imperial Majesty," said the old man, "begin with me."

The profound wisdom of this reply struck home at once. The emperor commanded that the stipends of all teachers should be instantly doubled. Soon the teachers were the wisest and best people in all the land and the emperor joyously ruled over the happiest and most prosperous people on earth.

Defending the Schools

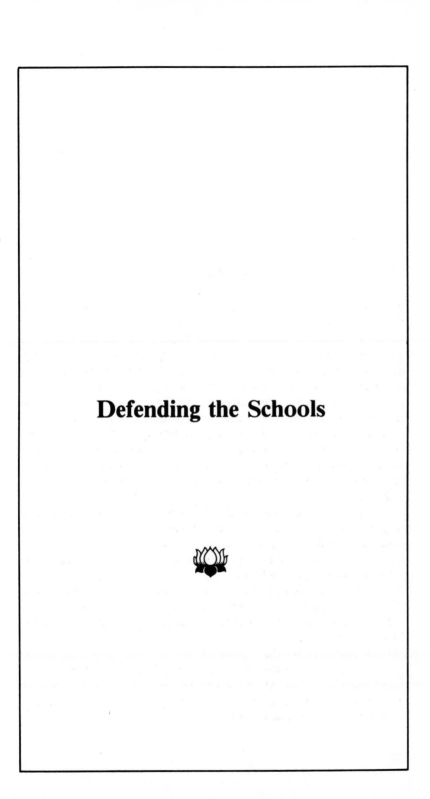

Criticism

If you want to criticize the schools to improve them rather than to destroy them, here are a few suggestions:

First, assume that the intentions of teachers are the same as yours. You may encounter an occasional exception, but teachers generally welcome frank comment. There is a legend that the pedagogue is complacent, timid, and tradition-bound. My experience with many thousands of teachers convinces me that, far from resting on past achievements, teachers are eager to experiment and improve.

Second, remember that the schools belong to the public. That includes you. You are entitled to comment on the school's work. You will do wisely to consider the advice of the professional staff, but the final decision rests with you and with your fellow-citizens. But not with you alone.

Third, see for yourself. When you select a car you don't send a neighbor to try it out. You go yourself because you think it is important. Visit your schools. It is not a social disgrace to consult a teacher. Do not rely on the reports of others, especially if those others are your own young children.

Fourth, expect change. If you find a school exactly like the one you think you remember from your own school days, you have found a rather poor school. Your children will spend most of their lives in the Twenty-first Century.

Fifth, get the facts. The supposed failure of the schools to get results has been alleged for many generations, including your own. Beware of angry generalizations. Most schools are doing a far better job now than when you were young. Fault-finding without fact-finding is sometimes fun but always futile.

"The Man with the Hoe"

L ively controversy continues over who should be educated and to what extent. Are there people who cannot benefit from education beyond the three Rs? The question is usually raised in a manner that suggests education happens only in a fixed span of time and that its content need not be related to the needs of the recipient. If an individual does not fit the educational program, the individual must change or fail.

However, the history of American education is a record of continuous efforts to alter the school to meet new personal and social circumstances. Man was not made for the Sabbath. Children are not born for the school.

So the issue about the distribution of education remains. Should the schools change further to accommodate different kinds of students? Some who feel that change has gone far enough also foresee frustration if we dangle before "ordinary" young citizens hopes that they may never attain. Why, they ask, offer cultural opportunities to those incapable of appreciating them? Why, to put it less elegantly, try to teach numbskulls more than the few skills they need to earn their daily bread? What to them are the wonders of science, the delights of the fine arts, "the long reaches of the peaks of song"?

The implications of selective educational distribution should awaken our deep distrust. Newton might have remained an unknown farmer and Pasteur a provincial mechanic without the impetus supplied by instruction. Failure to offer educational stimulus to the mute and inglorious creates a social loss which is large, continuing, cumulative, needless, and dangerous.

The Price Is Right

M uch of what we read and hear about taxes assumes that they are a form of compulsory charity. This is an error. Taxes are not alms. Taxes are the price of a public service.

It is easy to win public applause by presenting taxes as an expenditure for which the taxpayer receives no return except the momentary gratitude of public employees. If fact, however, citizens are not being robbed by a parasitic government. School services, developed by public demand, are supplied at a cost far less than the same services privately purchased.

With predictable regularity someone writes an indignant editorial announcing that citizens are required to work three months every year just to support government activity. By the same reasoning people have to work a month a year to support the automobile industry and several days to support the newspaper business.

Nothing is less mysterious, yet more confused, than expenditure for public objectives. Like private expenditures they may be well or badly managed. School taxes are the price of good schools. Ultimately, good schools cost less than poor ones.

No Second Chance

When hard times smite us, some people are sure to demand that expenditures for the schools be postponed until a better day. No fallacy about public education is more dangerous than the put-it-off hallucination. Education denied today is lost forever. The period of growing up never returns. There is no second chance.

Don't tell a youth, "Next year we shall build you a fine new school. Next year we shall see to instruction in health and safety. Next year we shall provide the best teaching and guidance staff in the state."

Next year, if we are lucky, that youth may be at work in a shop or factory. If we are unlucky he may be unemployed or confined in a reform school or appear in a morning police line-up.

Many other public expenses can be postponed — the new highway, the new street lights, the new car for the fire-chief. Delay will be an inconvenience but not a catastrophe. Education, however, is a continuous process and it must be provided continuously.

It has been said that justice delayed is justice denied. The same adage is equally true when applied to educational opportunity.

Two-Way Street

Most people think of the school superintendency as a unit in a chain of command. That image is accurate but incomplete.

We think of a line of authority and responsibility threading its way from the electorate down through the school boards and the administrators to the teachers and other school employees. It is true that ultimate authority for the public school system rests with the people, that instruction is provided by the teachers, and that the administrator is a transmission agent for the authority needed.

The image remains incomplete if the administrator transmits power in only one direction — down. The superintendent should also be an agent for transmitting ideas from teachers and others up to the school board and the community.

This second responsibility is as necessary as the first, but it is done less often and is more difficult to implement. The downward passage of authority might almost be performed by a machine; the second task clearly requires a sensitive and resourceful human being. An elevator with only a "Down" button would quickly end its run in the sub-basement, going nowhere from there.

What's Good About Our Schools?

A merican education is not, as some have implied, out of control and reeling from crisis to crisis. But it is a vast, complex, evolving phenomenon. As such, it has continuous problems, which all growing things create for themselves.

Along the road that American education has traversed there are many mileposts of substantial achievement. Yet educators rarely notice these signs of progress; instead, they stress the bumps, the sharp corners, tedious detours, and blind alleys along the road. At nearly every educational meeting, the educators tell each other—and the wide, wide world—all about their shortcomings.

I suppose it is wholesome that we fret about our failures and endeavor endlessly to make the good better. Yet, I wistfully trust that fine day will come when educators, and the public they serve, will be willing to count their blessings as well as their misfortunes.

In hopeful anticipation of that good day I offer for consideration six great assets of the American public school system.

1. It is controlled by the people.
2. It is administered by highly skilled professionals.
3. It enjoys sustained public interest and, with few exceptions, strong public support.
4. Its program is varied to meet the needs of local communities and their diverse populations.
5. It is served by skilled independent teachers.
6. It offers generous opportunity to all at public expense.

This list could easily be extended; the main point is that we should not worry so much about our problems that we forget our progress. Education is not a drifting ship. It has a precious cargo, powerful engines, and responsive professionals at the helm.

The Four Fears

I n an age of uncertainty all institutions come under attack and no target is more favored than the school system. Scared people flail out unreasonably in all directions and become "wrecking crews" of our schools.

Fear of change is a universal human trait. We are all more at ease amidst our comfortable habits. Indeed, a conservative tendency is a trait necessary to survival. However, fear of change is sometimes self-defeating. Some people who fear change have made the word "progressive," as applied to education, a term of reproach. Such extreme fear of change often betrays a lack of inner security.

Others of the wrecking crew simply *fear the results of education.* They doubt whether the masses are capable of learning. Extending educational opportunities to a broader population frightens them. They tend to favor a restricted curriculum, thus forcing many youths to withdraw from school. The concept of universal enlightenment evokes not enthusiasm but terror.

Another group has *financial fears.* The sociologists who studied *Middletown* found that, in nearly all local political issues, the only serious topic of discussion was the tax-rate. Many people judge most issues in terms of costs. The wrecking crews who assail our schools because "they neglect the fundamentals" or because the teachers are "too liberal" really use these accusations to cover a concern about their tax bill.

The final squad in the wrecking crew *fears subversion* in the schools. There have been social and economic changes in this country. The schools have helped to effect such changes. Major issues today often are fought first and most intensely in the schools. New sources of political power have emerged and former managers are being replaced. The wrecking crew easily enlists the displaced ones.

Faltering Allies

A child who attends school for 12 years spends over half his waking hours outside the school. The home and community exert more influence on the behavior of children than does the school. Government agencies, civic organizations, and other groups help to improve the community influence on children and youth. But if civic officials exploit public office and misuse public funds, if law enforcement is crippled by politics, if the police are venal and the courts corrupt, if parks, playgrounds, and libraries are starved for support, the best efforts of the schools to build character may be thwarted.

Many experienced teachers believe that TV and movies that deal lightly with homicide, cruelty, duplicity, and violence are responsible for some of their current difficulties. Neglect of home study, lack of sleep, and loss of interest in reading are also attributed by many teachers to the competing attractions of TV. Gory comic books and salacious newstand literature also share in the list of dishonorable mentions.

Most teachers would welcome more help to improve the community influences that condition their students' attitudes and behavior. Bad conduct, presented as normal or as morally neutral or even as heroic, makes the teacher's task more difficult and sometimes impossible.

The Public Schools: The Public's Schools

Because we all help to pay for the public schools, it is difficult, but necessary, to remember that since the schools belong to the public *collectively* they cannot be the property of any one of us or of any single group. Failure to observe this elemental fact is the basic cause of most of the school fights that supply much of the news about schools in the local press.

Yet how easily we all turn to the schools to promote our latest personal enthusiasms.

Do we want to build a bird bath in the city park? Let every child bring a dime to school next Monday and our project is financed overnight.

Since people behave in wicked ways and show a marked apathy toward church attendance, let us require our schools to open with prayer and daily Bible reading. We just can't see why the Supreme Court forbids such activity.

How about an impressive tree planting ceremony in honor of the Veterans of Foreign Wars? How charming to have 500 costumed school children stand in rows to form a living flag while the dedication addresses are delivered.

Push such multitudinous demands hard enough and you create a menace to the effective operation of a school program.

Discipline in Perspective

The greatest help in dealing with discipline, or the lack of it, is perspective.

Adults tend to forgive and forget their own youthful misdemeanors. Will Roger's remark, "Things ain't what they used to be—and probably they never wuz," is appropriate in any assessment of children by their elders. Forty centuries ago an Assyrian hacked out on a stone tablet his lament for the good old days when children were obedient, adding that the naughtiness of the little Assyrians probably presaged the end of the world. Since those ancient days each younger generation has seemed to its elders to be edging ever nearer to the snapping jaws of the dogs of doom. The dogs have had a long wait.

How to train young people in behavior deemed proper by their parents is a problem older than recorded history. Primitive tribes have initiated young people into adult status by means of painful, exhausting, blood-curdling rituals. The ancient Hebrews, advised by the Proverbs of Solomon, chastised their offspring, lest sparing the rod should spoil the child. In the schools of colonial America cruel and unusual punishments were inflicted for the slightest misbehavior: for failing to learn, the agonizing ridicule of the dunce's cap; for talking during lessons, the whispering stick, a split green twig into which the tongue of the offending child was clamped. If punishment and the fear of pain could turn the trick, the human race would have attained perfection long ago.

But all the beatings did not produce a single generation of giants in intellect or saints in conduct. Let us be clear, then, that we are not confronted by a generation of unusually bad or badly educated children.

If Johnny starts a free-for-all fight in the third grade, it doesn't solve the problem to know that his father and grandfather probably did likewise. But the perspective helps.

School Versus Community

The average American child attends school for less than 10,000 hours. During the other hours other influences take over. Some of the other influences help the school, some hinder it, some destroy its results as fast as they are achieved.

Schools teach healthful living; some families lack a good diet.

Schools nurture literary excellence; outside the schools printed pulp debases our children's speech and degrades their taste.

Schools teach honesty and respect for law; corrupt politics teach the opposite.

Schools teach temperance and moderation; many advertisements and much TV and the movies teach the opposite.

Schools teach the values of democracy; some aspects of life outside the school (and even at times within the school) negate and reject democracy.

Thus a society that proudly spends billions to support schools dedicated to lofty purposes requires, at the same time, that the schools divert much of their resources to repair the damage that the same society tolerates and even encourages. At best, the schools may help make boys and girls a little better than their parents. People who insist that the schools are permitting young people to avoid responsibility should remember that the disregard of social responsibility reaches its apex among adults.

War and Peace

Peace, Peace . . .

We shall not save succeeding generations from the scourge of war by conducting make-believe UN General Assemblies in our classrooms, or by memorizing the Preamble to the Charter of UNESCO, or by teaching children about their cute little Eskimo, Russian, Japanese, Mexican, or Ethiopian "cousins." Competence on international issues is not so easily created.

Teachers and curriculum experts may cry, "Peace, Peace!" at the top of their lungs and repeat the exercise 40 times a day. They may carry peace banners and picket in street demonstrations or at mass meetings. The goddess of peace will not heed such supplication.

If the discipline of school and home is based on fear and retribution, if the principal motive for learning is rivalry, if the chief object of education is personal advancement, if the atmosphere of school and neighborhood is heavy with intolerance and suspicion, if the life of the teacher is ignoble and shabby, if the bureaucracy of the school overwhelms the personalities of the children — then all the little peace campaigns will melt and run at the first hot touch of reality.

One other requirement: education for peace *in one country* is not safe. On this matter we cannot attend to only our own schools. If a small, weak country teaches aggression to its children, it offends the spirit of peace. If a powerful country teaches aggression, it makes the peaceful efforts of other countries counter productive.

The Perils of Irene

Those ancient Greeks showed great insight in establishing their pantheon. How significant it is that Irene, the goddess of peace, was the daughter of Zeus, god of power, and Artemis, goddess of justice!

The perils of Irene today arise more from weariness than from deliberate action. People become very busy. People forget. They forget what it cost in blood and tears and treasure to give us, the living, another chance to work for peace.

I see in this country, among teachers and the general public, marked relaxation in the drive for international peace. When the UN and UNESCO were created in 1945, we undoubtedly expected too much, too soon, too easily. For these over-expectations, all of us who had influence on public opinion must share responsibility. The UN system has not yet been able to exert effective international control over the forces of nationalism or to agree on what moral standards should guide the conduct of nation-states.

The task seemed in 1945 so much easier than it turned out to be. Having expected too much, it is easy to feel disappointed. Being disappointed, it is easy to despair. Irene, offspring of power and justice, is still in peril. But for Irene we know we must not and we will not despair.

Security

Because we believe that our nation may be threatened, we maintain a military establishment able to resist and (we hope) deter aggression.

Because we want peace, we try to establish conditions and relationships that will make peace possible.

The desire for peace and the desire for security are both intimately related to the system of public education.

The danger to the security of the United States is expected to last a long time—not just years but decades. Since the peril is protracted, the education of young people assumes greater importance.

The conflict is, in the main, a struggle for minds. Only people well-grounded in their own loyalties will be able either to protect the nation's ideals and the institutions which embody them or to win others to the cause of freedom.

In sheer numbers, the United States is at a substantial disadvantage. However, the outcome need not be determined in terms of massed manpower. Our great advantage is our industrial productivity. We can maintain this advantage by training loyal citizens and productive workers.

Thus three circumstances — the long duration of the confrontation, the fact that it is essentially a conflict of ideas, and that success need not depend solely on numbers — combine to stress the priority of education to national security.

Ivan

A ttending a school anywhere from Leningrad to Vladivostok, Ivan Ivanov learns many pleasant and useful things, just as other children do. He also learns that his motherland is beset by rapacious enemies. From the Bering Straits to the Baltic he learns that truth is what the state declares it to be. Every lesson is guided by a single system of thought, shielded from all other outside influences. Year after year Ivan learns to despise every element of independent thought. He has been systematically deafened to the thunder of reason or the whisper of conscience.

What then happens to Ivan? As a biologist he will be glad to submit his scientific integrity to the whims of a charlatan. As an historian he will cheerfully see to it that history conforms to the requirement of the party line. As a composer he will humbly ask whether his symphony is politically acceptable. All will submit, the brilliant and the stupid alike, to the directives of an omnipotent state.

There is something worse than such submission. Ivan will grow to maturity, live and die, and never know he lacks anything. Teaching for tyranny will so manage the credulity of childhood and the idealism of adolescence that the adult will never know what he has missed. Grim as it is to contemplate, realism requires us to note that this process now controls the education and the minds of a substantial portion of mankind.

Americans Abroad

T housands of American tourists and business people go abroad for work or pleasure. Few of them do anything, or are *asked* to do anything, that might promote international understanding. Few of them are well-enough informed to try.

My latest passport was delivered with a printed letter from the President exhorting me, in essence, to mind my manners while away from home. Since the letter was no doubt drafted to fit the needs and interests of every American going abroad, it was of little use. I think most travelers are ready, able, and willing to accept more substantial requests and suggestions.

The State Department has reams of unclassified material about political, economic, and social conditions in every part of the world. Much of this material is in published form.

Schools, colleges, libraries, and travel agencies might assist the American traveler to learn in advance about the countries he will visit. The international airlines, instead of presenting us Hollywood films which we can see at our neighborhood theater, might show us films about the land and the people to which they are carrying us.

It is even possible to hope that some tourists might continue to learn a little after they return home.

The most favorable time to learn is when motivation is high. For travelers abroad that time is just before and just after a visit. Much useful international understanding could thus be promoted at little cost.

A Whopper

The late General George C. Marshall once told a group of Cub Scouts that when he was a lad his circle of environment had a radius of only a mile or two. His sole contact with the U.S. Government was the rural post-office. He studied geography in school but he felt no personal relationship beyond the small community in which he lived.

Yet, during his distinguished lifetime, General Marshall was in direct contact with people in Tibet and Nepal, Paraguay and Uruguay, Iran and Iraq, Afghanistan and Pakistan.

"Far away places with strange-sounding names" became part of his daily routine. He was in touch with the great globe itself. What happened to General Marshall has in some degree happened to all of us in the last half-century. Only a few Americans remain who refuse to admit that the earth has grown smaller.

A certain boy, raised on an isolated farm, took his first trip to visit an uncle about 15 miles away in the nearest village. Musing on what to him was a dramatic experience, the boy exclaimed, "By golly, if the world is as big in t'other direction as it is over to Uncle Elmer's, she sure is a whopper."

It's all in the point of view.

Friends Abroad: Strength at Home

During World War II American teachers enlisted in a massive campaign of education to win the war and keep the peace. They secured amendments in the United Nations Charter providing for educational cooperation. They played the leading role in developing the charter and program of UNESCO. They lobbied for Senate approval of the UN Charter and for congressional funding for UNESCO.

They took the lead to create an effective world organization of the teaching profession. They worked for the passage of the Fulbright Act and other legislation for teacher exchange.

They established their own Overseas Teachers Fund that sent food, clothing, and medical supplies to teachers in the war-devastated areas, — for friends and former foes alike. They equipped whole sections of teachers' hospitals in Poland and the Philippines. They funded more than 100 teachers from abroad to travel and study in the United States. They sent 80 libraries of about 5000 books each to help students and teachers who had lost all their books in the war's devastation.

They diligently sought in their daily work in the classroom to develop sympathetic understanding of international problems.

Never in the history of education has a cause evoked more united, sustained, and devoted effort.

Now, a generation later, international good will still eludes us. Armed aggression has devasted large sections of Korea, Vietnam, and other countries. At many points force confronts force, and we await with foreboding the events of each new day.

What shall we conclude from this comparison of what was attempted with what has been attained? Were the efforts of the teachers to work for peace a naive, well-meaning blunder?

The search for peace has not been called off; it has been broadened. As far as the United States is concerned, the effort for peace now involves two additional requisites: national strength sufficient to deter aggression against us, and support from other free nations so that none of us need face possible aggression alone.

The schools can still help to achieve peace by helping to win friends abroad and to build strength at home.

A Few Questions and
Fewer Answers

Work as Education

Mahatma Gandhi considered economic productivity to be an essential part of education. Work, he believed, is the core of sound human development. In India work may occupy a central position in education because of the low economic level of the Indian population. However, the educational values of productive work need not be limited to the underdeveloped countries.

Whatever is economically necessary or useful can also be made educationally sound. Let our schools provide the educative benefits of productive work to all children and youth whether or not their own personal or family situations require work to produce income.

For instance, a small part of the physical and mental energy devoted to interscholastic football, say 20%, could, if devoted to productive work, do much more than provide goods and services badly needed in our personal and community economies. It would also produce lifelong educational advantages. It would ameliorate many of the problems of alienation and discipline that sorely trouble our schools today.

Labor omnia vincit—well, perhaps not *omnia* but a good deal anyway.

Partnership of Public and Private Schools

Partnership of public and private schools is not the same as co-existence. Partnership goes beyond antiseptic tolerance; it is a fruitful cooperation in order to meet a shared responsibility.

Some people refer to private schools as *independent* schools. This term, however, does not differentiate private schools from public. A church school is independent of the state. A state school is independent of the church. In both cases, complete independence is an illusion. There are important differences between public and private schools, but independence is not one of them.

Nine-tenths of all U.S. private schools are sponsored by the Catholic Church. They serve youth of a common religious creed. They belong to one cohesive, long-established, respected, and powerful church. Public schools, however, are governed by public bodies, responsible to people of widely different faiths as well as to people of no organized religious affiliation at all.

Partnership, I believe, is possible only if the basic differences between the partners are recognized *and accepted*. Each partner must have respect for the other. Neither must propose measures to threaten the existence of the other.

Archbishop James Ryan of Omaha once said: "Both the public schools and the private schools are here to stay. There is no reason why they should dissipate any of their effectiveness by constantly criticizing one another."

If that statement were worded as a prayer, a lot of people would gladly say "Amen" to it.

Two Sides of One Coin

There are two sides to the democratic process, just as there are two inseparable sides to a coin.

One side of the coin is the principle of *minority rights*. A dissident minority is entitled not just to a hearing but to a *listening*. There is a difference.

The majority is obligated to defer decisions until other viewpoints can be expressed and considered and is obligated not to ride roughshod over dissenting opinions. On most occasions, in my experience, we do quite well on this side of the coin. Allowing for lapses of human frailty, and with the help of the Bill of Rights, most organizations, including governmental units, do show respect for minority opinions and will go to considerable lengths to protect their utterance.

On the other side of the coin of the democratic process, our record is less praiseworthy. That other side of the coin is the principle of *majority decision*. We are not bound to accept a majority vote as personal conviction. Nor are we obliged to change our opinions because the majority disagrees with us. We are, nevertheless, bound by majority decision as a basis for concerted action. When free debate has been available, when the minority has been heard and the majority has spoken, the minority does not have the right to impede or sabotage majority decisions.

Decisions can always be reconsidered but they cannot be endlessly resisted. A successful democracy cannot prolong debate eternally. As we must not adopt majority opinions without hearing minority views, so we must not allow minority intransigence to nullify majority decisions.

Taxes

Ben Franklin spoke of the inevitability of death and taxes as if the two events were equally deplorable. His comparison is more epigrammatic than precise. There is such a thing as a tax refund.

Taxes are essentially a means to buy collectively what we cannot acquire individually. A good tax system is:

Adequate — providing revenue to meet government needs

Economical — cost of collection requires only a small part of revenue

Convenient — in terms of the place and time of payment

Flexible — capable of change to meet new circumstances

Diversified — different taxes to reach the varied forms of wealth

Fair — on the basis of two measures of equity in taxation: benefits received and ability to pay

One definition of fairness holds that each person should contribute to the support of government in proportion to benefits received. The gasoline tax is usually thus justified because the more one uses gas to drive on the highway, the more one pays in taxes. However, in most cases, it is difficult to tell how much benefit each taxpayer receives. Does a man with no children benefit from the education of other people's children? Suppose the childless man is connected with any aspect of the publishing business. General literacy is essential to his prosperity.

More broadly, it can be persuasively argued that education is so essential to public order that all citizens benefit from public schools. John Stuart Mill wrote that government is "so pre-eminently a concern of all, that to determine who are most interested is of no real importance." This is the basis on which ability to pay is held to be a better and more just criterion for taxation than benefits received.

Public Responsibility

I n all modern nation-states five basic services, without exception, are provided by action of the Government: foreign relations, national defense, law enforcement, postal service, and public education. Most governments provide many other services, too, but these five appear everywhere.

For public education the amount and character of the service vary from nation to nation, but some kind and amount of schooling is universal.

Adam Smith, the patron saint of free enterprise, believed in a narrow range of government functions. Defense and police he admitted as indispensable, along with a few other conveniences. Still the conservative author of *The Wealth of Nations* was a vigorous advocate of government providing education. The state should provide public education for what he called "the inferior ranks," because educated people were less inclined to disorder and more apt to give proper respect to their "lawful superiors." In a similar spirit an English writer declared, after the Second Reform Act of 1867, "Now we must educate our masters."

Until very recent times no one has seriously challenged the concept of public responsibility for education. Even today, with all our social earthquakes, the concept is assailed only rarely, unconvincingly, and feebly.

The most spectacular recent opposition was voiced in a book dictated in a Bavarian jail in 1924. In *Mein Kampf* Hitler rejected the concept of universal education as "a disintegrating poison invented by liberalism for its own destruction." He believed that most people were better off in the darkness of ignorance, illuminated at appropriate times by lightning flashes of propoganda. He regarded equal suffrage equal opportunity, and equal rights as "pernicious and destructive."

Apart from aberrations of this kind, the idea of public responsibility for education is firmly fixed. We discuss rationally not whether public education should be available but rather how and to what ends it should be directed.

The Foundation Shift

The private foundations wield a potent, but generally inconspicuous, influence. Authority to dispose of substantial sums of money is, always and inevitably, a source of power. The foundation administrator exerts an influence that has been steadily augmented in the past half-century.

The foundation executive, old-style, had self-imposed restraints on the use of power. To bestow or to deny financial support was a judgment required by his job. But, as a rule, he stopped at that point of decision.

The new-style administrator sees his responsibility in a different light and on a wider stage. He not only gives or withholds; he also supervises, evaluates, suggests, experiments, prods, coaxes, and restrains the objects of his generosity. By extensive use of matching requirements he can control the use not only of the money he provides but also of equal or greater amounts from private or public sources.

He is apt to equate novelty with wisdom. His test of the value of a project is whether he finds it "exciting." And he is rather easily bored. Headlong in pursuit of innovation, he finds current procedures weary, stale, flat, and unprofitable. He sometimes appears to be more eager to escape tedium than to establish the truth. He is profoundly skeptical of attempts to induce change from within existing institutions.

If he feels unable to trust anyone else to spend the foundation resources in a way that he deems acceptable, he may employ his own staff and conduct the project himself.

These shifts in the role of the foundations enhance their already substantial power. The exercise of that power is less accountable to public review than that of any other element in the complex of forces that produce change in American education today.

Education and National Development

Norway is a large moutainous rock, split with many openings that create scenic fiords. But it is covered, in the main, by a stingy, thin, and unyielding sod; its mining possibilities are limited; no major deposits of valuable ores have been found. In tropical Africa, in contrast, the land is lushly fertile and the area is the source of highly prized copper ores, gems, and uranium ores used to operate atomic reactors.

Norway has long had universal and effective public education. Tropical Africa has had nothing of the kind. The Norwegian people enjoy relatively high living standards, are cultured and healthy. By comparison, human life in tropical Africa is often short and living standards are at a subsistence level.

One can make many such comparisons: New Zealand and New Guinea; Switzerland and Bolivia; Japan and Madagascar. Even with limited natural resources, educated people produce and enjoy a good life. Nations bursting with natural riches but constricted in their educational opportunities have a low living standard.

This may not be conclusive evidence but, like the trout in the milk, it is highly suggestive.

The Heritage

The dominant theme of American education is the ideal of equal opportunity for all. Compared to this compelling theme, all others are merely orchestration and development. It is a great heritage.

Because of this heritage every child is born rich. He may not have the proverbial silver spoon. He has something better — a golden key, the key to unlock the door of opportunity. Americans have expected their public school system to produce miracles. In the past century the schools have not failed them. The schools have moved freedom forward, have helped to make the nation united, strong, prosperous, and free.

In these years, good times and hard times have alternated. The unity of the nation has been tested and affirmed in recovery from a civil war. Science and invention have revolutionized travel and communication. New materials, new power sources, and new medical discoveries have profoundly changed our personal habits, economic patterns, socio-political structures, and life expectancies. Wars of massive destruction and appalling ferocity have cast down some nations and created others.

Through all these upheavals the great heritage has continued to inspire our people. Barriers to equal opportunity have been removed and other barriers will fall in the future. We inherit, in this respect, not only the achievements of our predecessors but also their unfinished business.

The striving, too, is part of the heritage.

The Seed Corn

This nation could not long endure wrote the nineteenth-century British historian Thomas Macaulay to an American friend.

> I seriously apprehend that you will, in some such season of diversity as I have described, do things that will prevent prosperity from returning; that you will be like people who, in a year of scarcity, devour all their seed corn, and thus make the next year one not of scarcity but of absolute famine.

Macaulay had a low opinion of the self-discipline of large groups of ordinary people. He did not believe that the Americans could deny themselves present comforts in order to assure future necessities.

Neglecting the proper education of a single generation of youth is one way to devour the seed corn. The future security and well-being of the people depend, to a considerable degree, on their ability to perceive this danger. To this end, the American people need the partnership of the teaching profession. The people must be prepared, when necessary, to divert resources from the accumulation of goods to the building of citizens.

Walter Lippman, a decade after World War II, saw the same perils as did Macauley:

> How we feel entitled to treat our schools and our teachers . . . is still in approximately the same position as was the military effort before Pearl Harbor. . . . From being involved in wars for which we were inadequately prepared, we have acquired the will to defend ourselves. . . . Having acquired the will, we have found the way . . . even if we have to do without something else. In education we have not yet acquired that kind of will.

That summons to greatness still confronts us. Let us hope we never devour the seed corn. Oliver Goldsmith summarized the alternative very well:

> Ill fares the land, to hastening ills a prey,
> Where wealth accumulates, and men decay.

Bicentennial Thoughts

T he people who established this nation had no illusions about the risk they ran. They spoke gravely of lives, fortunes, and honor. They covered the peril of their efforts with the grim jest, "We must all hang together or we shall assuredly hang separately."

The achievement of independence through rebellion and the welding of 13 colonies into one nation through statesmanship called forth an enlightened and unselfish service never, perhaps, equalled in any other time and place.

Nationhood achieved, people turned their energies elsewhere. The epochs of continental and imperial expansion did not evoke a similar devotion to the public welfare. Aided by millions of immigrants, the resources of the nation were explored and exploited, coal in the Appalachians, gold in California, silver in the Rockies, lumber in the Northwest, oil in the Southwest.

Today we face the consequences of that methodical expansion. The days of easy citizenship are over. The future, always uncertain, is dark with foreboding, strewn with snares, paved with peril. We need again the commitment of high purpose and distinterested public service. This is a time to recall the lines George Washington speaks in Maxwell Anderson's *Valley Forge*:

> This Liberty will look easy by and by
> When nobody dies to get it.

Still It Is Not Treason

T he sensitivity of Americans to national security vacillates with the times. In the 1940s national magazines published many articles asserting that the schools sheltered disloyalty to the government of the United States. One such article stood out because of the shock of its title: "Treason in the Textbooks." I had at that time just completed a rather thorough survey of civic education. Thus prepared, I wrote a reply under the title, "This is NOT Treason."

In some ways the public mood today is similar to that of 1940. It may be useful to repeat the conclusion of my 1940 article. I believe it is still valid.

It Is Not Treason to Teach

—that American ideals require a fair chance for everyone in terms of economic, social, and educational opportunity;

—that these ideals are not yet fully achieved and to stir the enthusiasm of youth to attain these ideals more fully;

—that the current developments in our economic life put great strain on the institutions of democracy and to summon up youthful vigilance and courage to meet the challenge;

—that many different races and peoples have made a worthwhile contribution to the American culture;

—the importance of civil liberties and to give practice in using those liberties in dealing with debatable public questions;

—that the United States can learn some useful lessons from the experience of other countries;

—important truths, even though those truths be distasteful to powerful interests in the community; not treason yet, not yet in the United States of America.

The Best Weapon in the Arsenal

T he loyalty that citizens feel towards their institutions and to the moral principles undergirding these institutions is the strongest weapon in the nation's defensive arsenal. We may set a watch along all our borders, darken the skies with war planes, perfect our weaponry, and position our naval vessels along every mile of coastline. Even then we are unsafe unless the Americans think seriously and care deeply about their civil liberties and civic responsibilities.

An informed and active loyalty is the keystone of national defense. Without it, every weapon detracts from our strength. Other governments may seek to confirm their national unity by control of the press, or by a state religion, or by repressive military power, or by other tyrannies. But such methods are alien to the American spirit and will remain ineffective.

We require a loyalty freely given but not commanded, intelligent because it is informed, active because it has often been practiced in home and school.

We do not inherit democratic values as we inherit dark eyes or curly hair. We learn them. No one ever learned to swim by standing on dry land and memorizing the rules of swimming. One can sink like a rock even if one can list the values of swimming as a form of exercise. We learn to be loyal just as we learn other things, not by accident, not by good intentions, but by purposeful continued practice under skilled and stimulating guidance.

America: The Beautiful?

Few pleasures excel vindication. "I told you so," is one of the most gratifying expressions in the language. So I will repeat below the gist of a statement I made over thirty years ago—in September 1947, to be exact:

I love thy rocks and rills
Thy woods and templed hills

Thus runs the national song. Millions of school children sing it every day. But what can these words mean to them? To a considerable portion of our people the scenic grandeur of America means nothing but a chance to make money. Outside of a few national and state parks, accessible beauty spots are being systematically destroyed. Highways invade the land with hard, wide strips of asphalt, gasoline fumes, and danger. Garish advertising signs cut off the view by day; at night the neon chokes out the stars and the moon. Litter accumulates, streams and lakes are polluted, loudspeakers shatter the rural silence with appeals to attend the ball game or ride the speedboat. The utter lack of taste of most roadside businesses is a constant and needless offense to the eye.

We have been inexpressibly careless about our heritage of national scenic beauty. Perhaps we had too much of it to begin with. But unless remedial measures are taken soon, the time of reckoning will come. As the children sing their songs about their country, it would be well to examine what is happening to the environment of their own communities. Perhaps a new generation, educated to respect and appreciate nature, will be more wisely protective than its predecessors. End of 1947 remarks. I told you so.

Gratuitous Advice

Start to Finish

The above title should be read as an imperative sentence — an exhortation if not a command.

The great waste of time and energy is not inertia, but rather impulsive and unexamined enthusiasms. We squander our limited resources by starting too many things we never finish.

Examples of this profligacy are everywhere. The new filing system that was never quite ready to use; the daily diary that languished after two weeks of effort; the rock-garden half built; the book manuscript in the dusty bottom drawer lacking only the three final chapters; the personal budget system ceremoniously launched in January and secretly abandoned in mid-April; the letter to an old friend (it could be finished in 10 minutes although it was begun six months ago); the plan for a systematic self-improving program of reading; the hopeful self-instruction in Spanish that taught only too well the meaning of "mañana." Each of us can add his own examples to the list.

Complete what you begin. Start only what you really intend to finish. Rash and ill-considered beginnings lead only to profitless and dreary conclusions.

Concentrate and Persevere

Two great strategic principles determine the success of individuals or organizations.

The first principle is that of concentration of effort on a few limited but highly significant objects. The manpower and the resources must be poured into a few efforts in order to make a crucial difference in the outcome. Strength does not arise from the unplanned dispersal of small efforts.

The second principle is perseverance. The proverb proclaims that "well-begun is half-done." True enough; but half-done is in itself of little value. No one yet has put his name in the history books by sailing half-way to the New World, or by climbing half-way up Mount Everest, or by a remarkable time in the first 50 yards of a 100-yard dash.

Bending an ordinary iron bar illustrates both strategic principles. If you raise its temperature by one degree, it will not bend. Increase that by a second degree and it still remains rigid. The temptation is strong to conclude that heat does not make iron pliable. After a blacksmith applies enough heat at one point the white hot iron will sag limply over the anvil and the workman can tie a knot in it. It was not the one final degree of heat that made the iron bend; it was the concentration of much heat at one point in space and time.

Projects launched with modest hopes, tentative goals, and faint finances are unlikely to succeed. Projects of great moment require bold and massive plans. This is the approach which painted the Sistine Chapel, unlocked the atom, and put men on the moon.

Cynicism and despair are the product of small resources briefly applied to great enterprises. It is sometimes worse to exert nearly but not quite enough effort than to make no effort at all.

Time Out

O nce upon a time an enthusiastic angler became president of a large university. He asked an older and more experienced university president for advice on how to succeed as president and still have time to satisfy his interest in fishing.

"Your problem," replied the older man, "is not very complex. First, you must get enough money to operate the university. Then you must recruit a staff sufficient in numbers, wisdom, and ability to serve all the students on campus. As soon as you have taken these two simple steps, you may go fishing."

Charged with zeal, the young president plunged into his task. One day he decide that he could go fishing. Gear in hand, he headed for his favorite stream. He was, however, unable to find the stream. All the landmarks were changed. He asked an old man, "Where is Willow Creek?"

"You're too late," he replied, "that stream has been dried up for 30 years."

A university president should go fishing before the chores are all done, before the alumni discover that his presence in the stadium does not guarantee victory in the home-coming game, before the anarchical tendencies that simmer just below the surface in every college faculty erupt in full vigor, before the deans discover that he will not double the budget of each department each year, before the parents realize that the president is not personally acquainted with every freshman on campus, before the students discover that his stern eye cannot really detect their innermost thoughts—long before that, let the president take time out to go fishing.

Even a Star Needs an Understudy

In Napoleon's army, so it is said, every foot soldier carried in his field knapsack a marshal's baton, just in case he might suddenly be called upon to assume supreme command over the French armed forces. The legend is true only in a figurative sense, but the lesson of the legend is as solid truth as one can speak. No major enterprise can operate well or long on the theory of the indispensable man.

Such administrators as school superintendents and college presidents should stuff many symbolic batons into knapsacks of subordinates. The lack of enough batons in enough knapsacks can ultimately create failure for an administrator whose other policies are beyond reproach.

When Herbert Weet retired as school superintendent in Rochester after a long career of exceptional service, one of his admirers asked him how Rochester could possibly manage without him. His response helped to explain his success. He said, "To discover how indispensable anyone is, thrust your hand into a bucket of water and then find the hole when you withdraw your hand." It is a wise policy to have a qualified understudy ready to fill any break in the ranks wherever it may occur—including the top job itself.

Problems and Options

When you encounter a major problem, you may react to it in one of four ways.

You may say, "Yes, I'm worried, but I don't like to fret or have others think me inadequate. I will thrust this problem from my mind. I hereby declare that it does not exist." Then you strive to "think positively," to forget the problem, and to wait patiently for a miraculous self-solution.

Or you may say, "This is indeed a real problem. It does bother me. However, I don't want to tackle it just now." Like Scarlett O'Hara you decide to "think about it tomorrow."

Or you may say, "This problem gives me no rest. I shall do something about it now. Even if I don't deal with it correctly, that will be better than doing nothing." So, like the oyster with an irritating grain of sand, you work all alone and secretly to build a pearl around your trouble.

There is a fourth option. It is usually the most effective one. You can say, "I must consult with other more experienced people to help me decide what to do."

Option four appears to be so much more time-consuming than the others. Worse, it requires you to admit your own fallibility. That is one big reason why so many people have unsolved problems.

Fame or Power

S weet are the attentions of publicity; bitter are the fruits of notoriety. Many proclaim that they desire no personal fame, but few there be who can resist its allurements. It builds prestige and inflates the ego. How sweet it is!

The administrator, in his unavoidable daily contact with the press and other media, has to walk a narrow path between anonymity and renown.

If he shrinks too deeply into the background, he may find himself without a platform when some major crisis arises. If he is too assiduous in getting his name into print, he will almost certainly diminish his usefulness.

Benjamin Jowett, whose students at Oxford included a remarkable number of men who rose to political prominence in England, used to warn them: "It is most important in this world to be pushing, but fatal to seem so."

By and large, the more good publicity that can be attached to an institution, the better; the less publicity that can be acquired by an individual, the better. Few of us can enjoy both influence and fame. It is usually necessary to choose between them.